WOMEN

AND

Wealth

Dr. Patricia K. Laino
SUCCESSFUL WOMAN ENTREPRENEUR

Printed in the United States of America.

ISBN 1-4196-1390-1

Published by
BookSurge, LLC
5341 Dorchester Road, Suite 16
Charleston, SC 29418
1-866-308-6235

Acknowledgements

My deepest appreciation is given to my editor, Dr. Arthur Seamans and his talented assistants, April Anderson and Dominic Tarantino. Dr. Seamans's magical editorial touch enhanced my work to the highest degree beyond anything that I could have ever imagined and I truly thank him and his associates for their priceless assistance.

I'm indeed indebted to my publisher and the dedication and support of the entire staff for making this publication a reality. A special thanks to Becky Bayne for designing the unique and artistic cover. I would also like to extend a sincere thank you to Barbara Goldsmith for her creative photography.

My family understands the importance of my work and more specifically my need to write for women who want to become successful entrepreneurs. I would like to give a special thanks to my children and grandchildren who have been very supportive every step of the way in my research and writing.

Preface

Imagine that you could have a conversation with the most successful women entrepreneurs in the world about starting your own business. Well this book covers just that! The most successful women entrepreneurs in the world seem to have very little in common. Yet despite their differences, they do share one common trait, which is their strong belief that they will succeed no matter what obstacles get in their way. Once they set their mind on starting their own business, they do not hesitate to move on with a passion unsurpassed by anyone or anything. Their belief is so strong that they tend to excel in every situation. They set their expectations high and raise the bar any opportunity that comes their way. They motivate those around them, set the right goals and objectives and let nothing get in their way to achieving success in business. Six figure women have a habit of freeing up new and unique strategies that allow them to thrive and grow. They find their customers; take exceptional care of them and link productivity and profits to total customer satisfaction.

The philosophy of *Women & Wealth* is to prepare women to put into action a way of life to start-up and operate a business never before imagined. You will be prepared to accumulate wealth in abundance when applying the secrets used by the most successful women entrepreneurs around. This text contains successful and unique strategies, after having been put to practical tests by hundreds of aspiring women entrepreneurs from all walks of life. Many of these women have gone on to become some of the most successful entrepreneurs on record.

It is my hope, as the author, to help ease the thorny path of starting your own business as a woman in today's entrepreneurial arena. It's not easy becoming an entrepreneur and it's even more difficult if you are a woman. Why do women have such a hard time starting up and making a success of their own business?

I have asked myself this question thousands of times over the past decade while teaching, coaching and mentoring an array of aspiring women entrepreneurs of all races, color, nationalities and income levels. The book will identify both the strengths and weaknesses of thousands of women who have pursued opening their own businesses. Best of all, this book will show you how to apply the secret skills to achieve your own entrepreneurial success.

This text is user friendly and each chapter identifies and describes in plain language the general concepts concerning businesses in general and successful businesses in particular. There is a common theme that runs throughout the practical tips in this book – the need for a Business Action Plan that works and the skills to successfully implement it! In addition, hundreds of tips are here that will help you avoid failure and spur you on to your own business success.

Early on, I learned that women fall into one of two categories; those who succeed and make money, and those who just "tread water" and never really thrive or succeed in their business venture.

The focus of this book is on two women who represent the successful entrepreneur called Victoria and the less fortunate woman called Losera and their journey of starting their own businesses.

The overall mission of this text is to identify the characteristics of Victoria and Losera, describe their traits and their travel on the road to success, identify why some female entrepreneurs falter and some succeed in business and how to develop the ultimate Business Action Plan for your own success.

Unless your business is making a profit, then it is my opinion that it not successful. This rationale sounds simple, but I can tell you that I have seen hundreds of entrepreneurial women counting on someone else to pay their basic bills time and time again. Perhaps, what they should do is go to work for someone else. The journals I have retained through the years reveal many traits of the successful women and the not so successful women who want to become entrepreneurs. My mission in writing this book is to share with you why some women become six figure earners (Victoria) and others (Losera) struggle to pay their basic bills.

This book will give all women who read it the insight, exposure to unique skills and wisdom to go on to become successful as Victoria. This book details the very start of the business adventure by Victoria… how it was conceived, born, thrived, struggled, grew and lived on. This is Victoria's Profile that spans how she envisioned, created and launched her own business, made money and became wealthy beyond all expectations. Victoria did this by following the easy-to-adopt profit-generating steps and the associated actions that she took to avoid failure.

This book challenges the basic ideas about starting your own business. It brings a powerful and true model called the Business Action Plan, complete with specific actions that become the keys to succeeding in business. In every chapter of this text, notes have been made on the specific traits that hundreds of women like

Victoria have demonstrated in their unshakable search for success. These are the women who went on to develop their Business Action Plan that brought them happiness, wealth and earned them the aura of Victoria.

Table of Contents

Introduction

You are probably wondering why this is a book just for women. My experience with women entrepreneurs has led me to believe that women are truly unique when it comes to starting a business. The interactions that I have had with thousands of women have prompted me to write this book to inform the readers about how women differ from men and other women. It will give you insight about what it takes to succeed in business as a woman.

This book carries you through the live experiences that women encounter while trying to open a business. It will take you down the road that only women travel to get to their final destination place called business success. This book is not about gender, but about how a woman differs from a man who travels the same road. Men are welcome to read this book and perhaps they too will discover some hints and ideas along the way to enhance their own business success.

Most women lack an old boys or old girls network to help them succeed in business. Many wear too many hats to really get serious about starting their own business. They are very caring individuals who put their family and children first. Now this is acceptable, but starting a business requires long hours and complete dedication. In order for a woman to succeed, she must search her soul to be certain she is ready to make the sacrifices that need to be made to launch her business.

Through the centuries men have been the designated breadwinners and sole providers for their families. These roles have been passed down through time whereby men are taught specific survival skills needed in the business world. Many women have difficulty with becoming the breadwinner because they have not been conditioned to doing so. I find that many women become dependent upon someone else to help finance their business operation to the extent that they can't survive without him or her.

Most men have thick skin and let things roll off their back, whereas women tend to be emotional and have fear of making someone angry. I believe that you can't be powerful if you never engage in conflict situations that frequently arise when starting up a business. Successful women are willing to address conflict situations as they arise because to avoid conflict means giving up power to your opponents.

Many women are reluctant to make money, and I call this the fear of financial success. It took me many years and a great deal of research to determine that many women think being poor is noble and giving away their product or service relieves the guilt they feel of becoming prosperous. Early on in my career, I was one of these women, but a six-week course called *God in Money* changed my direction and ultimately enabled my success in business. I came to realize that the more money my company made, the more people I could hire, and the more wealth I could spread around. Successful women, including me, believe that money buys them freedom and independence.

I have found that most successful women challenge change head on and take changes as opportunities instead of threats.

Going into business for most women is like going into the desert alone. They lack a strong network to help them secure business resources. They are alone without help from the network that men usually rely upon for business comfort and security. They have few options for facing unending challenges. Therefore, they have a feeling of emptiness. The successful women look for an oasis in the desert. Through belief, they find that restorative place by networking and seeking, finding, and using solutions. The successful women ask, seek, and secure help. They have unfathomable belief in their business success.

Through the years I have seen the most unlikely women succeed in business by their strong belief in their success. I never hear them say, "I can't do this, and I can't do that." The successful women go on to develop their Business Action Plan. Because they have such effective selling skills, financial institutions eventually invest in the company and enable them to make money.

This book will help women in their travels through the startup maze by giving them total entrepreneurial skills for success not readily found in other books. Through the examples of successful and not successful women, we will discover the basis for a successful entrepreneur operation. No other author could guide you through these scenarios because first hand experiences are my key to bringing clear-cut reality to the reader. The successful women have a vision of exactly what their business will be and what it will look like. The unsuccessful women will demonstrate naiveté and surrender their future to fear, doubt, and lack of belief in their ability to succeed.

Going into your own business will change your thinking and your life forever! Whether you plan on opening a gift shop, pizzeria, cleaning service, or a high tech shop, you should take specific actions before you legally sell your products or services. Throughout this book you will follow the path that Victoria takes to achieving business success and Losera, who falters and loses her quest of starting her own business. We will highlight Victoria, who rises to success, and Losera, who falls by the wayside.

Victoria is not an ordinary woman, but an extraordinary individual who carries her unique qualities and skills into creating a profitable business venture. Victoria is like an artist who crafts a Business Action Plan as her masterpiece. She paints it with love and a sense of anticipation, and her business thrives as a result of her uniqueness. When you ask Victoria about her business, she emphatically states that it will be a colossal success; she has not doubt in her mind.

Losera is a woman who usually starts her business without knowing who her customers are and whether or not this business could really be a success. Seldom does she complete a Business Action Plan, but operates by the seat of her pants. Unconsciously, she frowns upon making money.

The mission of this text is to point you in the right direction as you begin your travels through the world of owning and operating your very own successful business. It will take you through the red tape of startup and take the secret out of successfully becoming a Victoria. It outlines all of the basic points for developing your Business Action Plan (BAP) that becomes your roadmap to success. This text will also highlight the path that Losera takes in starting her business, making you aware of all the obstacles and pitfalls that get in your way when you are developing your BAP.

As a woman entering the world of entrepreneurship, you are going to be a part of the gigantic wave that's growing in size and sweeping across America. Many business researchers predict that in the future approximately 60% of all new innovations and changes will come from women like you and me in the business arena throughout our nation and the world.

While numerous major businesses and Fortune 500 companies are closing their doors, downsizing and becoming lean and mean, thousands of new women businesses are emerging. In the year 2010, it is projected that approximately 85% of all working people will be employed by small businesses, and women will own half of these businesses (United States Department of Labor, 2002).

Many, like yourself, feel lost in the wilderness of going into business, not realizing that advice and support are available to you. All that you need to know is what there is readily available and where to look for it. There are entrepreneur centers and women's business centers like ours, libraries, and business workshops and seminars that can get you started in your business planning. However, there is no author as candid and full of hints as I am.

I have often wondered what compelled me to write this book, and a multitude of reasons began to surface. On a Saturday morning in March, 2005, I finally gathered all of these reasons together. The true motive of why I wrote this book became clear. This book had to be published for all the women out there who want to start their own successful business and need what it takes to step out of the shadows and into the light of their own business success.

My father died when I was two years old, and my mother brought up five children by working two jobs as a cleaning woman. One of the houses she cleaned was the home of a famous violinist. She cleaned the house in exchange for violin lessons for me. Since my mother's workdays were twelve to fourteen hours long, we children took care of running the entire house.

I was brought up in a home that was very happy because we didn't really know that we were poor. I think that makes a difference in your outlook on life. We never owned a home or car, but all it took was a Sunday ride offered by our neighbors to make us happy. I still keep in touch with some of the friends from my childhood. Many have gone on to become highly successful people, and I conclude that their success was due to their commitment to hard work.

My mother was the most influential person in my life because she always told me that I could do anything in my life that I wanted to and money didn't make the difference. Initially, she wanted me to follow in the footsteps of my violin instructor and play in a symphony orchestra, but my passion for this was lacking. I graduated from high school, won a scholarship to go to the local nursing school, practiced as a surgical nurse for five years, and went on to teach nursing for five years. In the midst of beginning my career, I married and my husband and I raised two wonderful children.

It never occurred to me that I would fail at anything that I put my mind to doing. Some will say such optimism is stupid and others will cry, "Go for it. What do you have to lose?" My positive attitude keeps me eager to accept changes and challenges as just more mountains to climb on my journey to success. In this book I will share my secrets to business success and those secrets of women who have crossed my path throughout the years. I concluded that this book would become the means of reaching thousands more women in order to make their journey to business success a little easier.

When I was an instructor of nursing, the emotion laden and structured hospital life began to bother me. It was then that I decided that I wanted to do something different with my life. I talked it over with my husband and children, and they agreed that it would be a good idea to go back to college and obtain new skills. Further education changed my life forever.

While in college, I enrolled in a creativity class. One day, the professor asked us what we wanted to do with the rest of our life. She pointed to every student, and when she came to me, I blurted out, "I want to start my own business." Where this wish came from, I'll never know, but probably it originated in my subconscious mind.

The idea of starting my own business remained dormant until I found the need for additional money to supplement my college costs. I started conducting workshops on the subject of handling stress that I had researched and studied, both at the undergraduate and graduate level. My doctoral advisory committee said that I shouldn't pursue the subject of stress because it wasn't measurable, and, therefore, it would take me forever to complete my doctoral studies. I knew that doing research on the subject of stress would reinforce my expertise for conducting future stress workshops, and, therefore, would attract more customers. Accepting this challenge proved its worth because it culminated with one of the first doctoral dissertations on stress being accepted at the University of Buffalo.

After my graduation, it was natural to continue with the stress workshops. The customers were coming to me, and the pay was attractive. I made the decision to open my own stress management company. Since I had no idea how to start this business, I began seeking advice. Because there were few who could and would help me to start this venture, I started keeping a diary of events about what it took to start this business. Knowing failure wasn't an option, I ensured my success by focusing on finding customers and making money. Later my diary became the basis for this book (but I'm getting ahead of myself here).

When I opened my very first home-based business, family members became my mentors. Primarily, I turn to them in times of need for advice, but I have also added other mentors along the way. The first business was called Bio-Lain Research, and it seemed like a good business name until one of my customers who received my brochure thought that it was the answer to her Pap smear test. After brainstorming with the family, I quickly changed the name to Life Masters. To save money, I had my family design and produce my first business cards and brochures.

Soon I was off and running as an entrepreneur, and everything appeared to be going along well during the first few months. I needed to conduct only one Stress Workshop a month to cover all of my monthly overhead expenses. All of the additional workshops were net profits, I thought! The poet Thomas Gray used the phrase "ignorance is bliss," and how true the saying was. I never thought or knew about putting some money aside for taxes, travel, additional handouts for big crowds, hiring some extra help and writing my car off as a business expense.

My business continued as usual, until it started producing excess profits. I surmised that it was time to set up a business account to separate my business and personal monies, so I called a friend in banking. She said to come into the bank and bring my DBA. When I asked her what the DBA was, she said, "Oh no! Just come in as soon as possible." The next day, I discovered that a DBA was the Doing Business As form that you file with the local county clerk when you start your business, and so I filed mine the next day, after being in business over four months. It was just another learning experience.

Everything else associated with my business venture seemed to be falling into place until I signed a contract for fifteen stress workshops with New York Telephone Company. Until then, all of my workshops had been one day long, and the customer would pay me at the end of the workshop. After three weeks of completing six AT&T workshops, I hadn't received a single check. When I called my AT&T contact, she asked me where I had sent the bill. Boy, did I think fast, and said that though the bill was waiting to be sent, I needed the billing person's name and address. I had no idea how to put together a voucher, much less have the form. Consequently, I ran to the local stationary store and asked the manager for help. After she sold me generic vouchers, I sent them in. Finally, I got paid. I didn't consider this a mistake because I didn't know any better; it was just another learning experience.

These obstacles that arose didn't discourage me because I learned to call them learning experiences. These adventures in starting my own business became a long string of learning experiences.

As the customer list grew and more money was coming in, I thought it was time to hire someone to help with the bookkeeping. This bookkeeper set up a most simple method, but within one year, we outgrew this system. My mentor Dorothy suggested that I contract with a Certified Public Accountant (CPA) firm. I took her advice and added the CPA firm to my advisory team. Even though I had acquired a CPA partner, Dorothy continued to be my mentor on financial issues until her untimely death.

Still home-based, the Life Master Program had to be expanded because once I conducted a stress workshop for my customers, they wanted something new and different. These desires resulted in the creation of over fifteen new workshops during the next year. These workshops ranged from time management to effective communications, strategic planning, marketing and advertising, and customerization. I held these workshops throughout the country.

During year two, my husband's illness caused me to restrict my travels. It became apparent that Life Masters had to be put on hold and was even in jeopardy. A position at the local college was announced in the newspaper. After I applied, I was hired as Director of the Entrepreneur Division.

I thought that I could do both the consultant business and this job in order to meet the skyrocketing bills resulting from my husband's illness. It quickly became evident that I missed and longed for the freedom to give exclusive attention to my own business. Could I not make all the money that I needed in my own business? The major obstacle to resuming my business venture was that I was unable to do extensive travel, and this problem had to be quickly resolved. After a brainstorming meeting with my mentors, the suggestion was made to bring customers to me instead of my going to them. Eureka! This idea was to change my life.

I looked at my diaries which recorded the coping strategies I used to overcome the trials. From these entries, I developed a new business plan. This new plan was the basis for setting up workshops in a location other than my house. With my new plan completed, I located an affordable site within an incubator. This was a place where small companies like mine could stay for three years. Tenants shared services and were charged extremely low rent because this incubator was New York State funded. When I signed the lease and had sufficient customers contracted for workshops, I resigned from the college. The training center that I had dreamed of was now becoming a reality. This new center needed a new business name that would match its mission. My mentor attorney recommended that it be incorporated to give this business credibility and to protect my assets. My mentors then suggested the organization be called the Business Training Institute.

Our Senator and Mayor cut the ribbon for the grand opening. Initially, I hired two extremely efficient employees (who are still with me), and we began to offer all of the previous business and management workshops here at the center.

Though the business was doing well, I still had the desire to focus helping women like me who wanted to start their own business. In my spare time, I began writing a curriculum that would teach women how to open and operate their own successful business by using specific methods. Developing this curriculum was easy for three reasons: first, I had the expertise in writing curriculum that I learned in college; second, I had the diaries on setting up businesses; and third, I had a burning passion to write this.

Shortly after I completed the curriculum, opportunely, three major companies and Griffiss Air Force Base closed, which terminated over seven thousand jobs in our region. These closures became a tremendous opportunity to turn lemons into lemonade by teaching the talented dislocated workers about how to start their own business.

Now there was a need for funding to implement this new plan. After I went to my local lawmakers to launch the idea of how to create new jobs with our specific training, they agreed to furnish a one-time grant. Setting up this training was not without real problems.

At the time, the 100-hour training program was conducted once a week for three hours for twenty participants. It took nine months for participants to complete the program.

The problem was how we were going to train over two hundred dislocated workers with only three instructors available. Immediately I called a meeting with all of my mentors. One mentor was a creative visionary, and I knew that if I ever needed her to come up with creative ways to do the training it had to be then. She didn't seem the least bit concerned about our worry of not being able to handle all of these people. She offered two solutions: first, offer the 100-hour training program for seven hours each weekday, allowing the program to be completed in three weeks; and second, offer the 100-hour program for three and a half hours during evenings, allowing the program to be completed in six weeks. She recommended that we double the class size and have two instructors in case one couldn't make a class or was ill.

Everyone thought it couldn't be done because the participants would never agree to these long hours, and we didn't have enough instructors. She held fast by mentioning that the participants had been working eight hours a day and were now laid off and doing nothing. "Why not have them come here for a workday of training and graduate them in three or six weeks instead of the current nine months?" she asked. She made it sound so simple that we all bought into the concept, asking her for more advice. The next problem was how we would secure at least eight new instructors. She suggested that we could employ our previous graduates who had finished our training program, completed their BAP, and knew that the program really worked.

Immediately we hired and trained new instructors. After the programs were completed, many of our participants went on to open new businesses. Additional grant funds began to come to us because of our successful track record for training at such a rapid speed. Soon after, one of my mentors informed me grants were being awarded to create new Entrepreneur Assistance Centers (EAC) throughout New York State. Our own training program was exactly what these centers would be designed to do. I submitted a proposal to create a center in our incubator, and three months later we were granted the funds. Three months later, I was awarded this grant to establish the first EAC here in the Incubator to serve the three surrounding counties. Since then, we have received new funding every year because of our outstanding track record. We have been recognized as the #1 center in the state for over ten years with hundreds of training programs and thousands of graduates.

To accommodate our expansions, our CPA firm recommended that we add our own in-house finance division. The CPA firm assisted in selecting the personnel for this division.

Everything was going so well within the incubator, that we needed more training space. Our landlord agreed to move our center into a large site for a reasonable rent. We moved to the new site, but in year two, the exterior of the whole incubator site was beginning to deteriorate. This deterioration reflected poorly on our image. This was unacceptable because we will only be first class in our appearance.

On a business trip to Buffalo, New York, my staff and I were given a tour of a new wing that was being added to a classy downtown hotel. We saw that a physician, insurance agent, financial planner, and other professionals were going to lease space in this new addition. After returning home, we immediately set up a meeting with the manager of the most outstanding hotel and conference center in our city. We wanted to know whether or not there was any site within this property that we could lease. The manager arranged for me to meet with the two owners the very next week. The focus of my presentation included a mention of the benefits that they would realize if they leased to us. These benefits included increased customers for dining and lodging. It would also bring hundreds of new people into their hotel. I promised that I would personally recommend their hotel to all my clients and business contacts. They agreed to lease us the entire front section of their facilities. In addition, they offered to assume the costs of the renovations.

Our grand opening, sponsored by the hotel, turned out to be magnificent. Business people from all over the state attended and toured our state-of-the-art facilities. We were to become an outstanding showcase of a successful business in the heart of our inner city. Three years later, in the fall of 2000, the state announced that it was receiving proposals to establish a federally funded Women's Business Center (WBC) to serve all of upstate New York. I knew this was my opportunity to shift my focus to helping women. The targeted region was so vast that we could expand beyond our wildest imagination.

Our center won this award, and in June, 2001, the grand opening of the first Women's Business Center of New York State was held. Congressmen, the regional SBA Director, Mayors, County Executives and other dignitaries were all in attendance. Since its inception, this WBC has been recognized as one of the most outstanding Women's Business Center in the nation.

Other opportunities for our center continue to arise. We plan to remain a million dollar-a-year plus enterprise long into the future. In addition, all of my employees are cross-trained to improve their performance and maintain the operations with continuity.

Even though my capable staff could do the work without me, I don't want to retire because I have too many mountains left to climb. I think hard work is good for me. As my friend Carl Eilenberg recently wrote about me in his newspaper, "She feels twenty, looks forty and that's all you need to know!"

Traits of a Victoria
By the Author

1. Strong Belief In Her Success
2. Listener
3. Sense of Humor
4. Positive Thinker
5. Creative Mind
6. Loves Making Money
7. Effective Communicator
8. Doer
9. Change Agent
10. Loves Life
11. Sense of Wonderment
12. Focuscd
13. Leader
14. Calculated Risk Taker
15. Young At Heart
16. Honest
17. Problem Solver
18. Expects Nothing But The Best
19. Motivator
20. Forgives & Forgets
21. Super Seller
22. Happy Attitude
23. Goes For The Gold
24. Analytical
25. Logical
26. Feels Lucky
27. Motivated
28. Shares
29. Does The Impossible
30. Takes Action
31. Team Player
32. Independent Thinker
33. Decision Maker
34. Organized
35. Delegates
36. Good Friend
37. High Spirited
38. Time Manager
39. Feels That She Will Never fail
40. Daring
41. Trend Setter
42. Manages Stress
43. Sense Of Wellness
44. Makes Things Happen
45. Consults With The Masters
46. Produces Miracles
47. Planner
48. Meshes Work & Play

CHAPTER ONE
Assessing the Nature of the Winning Business Woman

Before you think about launching a business, it is important to evaluate your own strengths and weaknesses and begin to shape yourself into the kind of businesswoman that you'd like to be. After all, the kind of person you are is key to the success of the business you propose to create. If you wish to become a Victoria, you will need to emulate her qualities. If you wish to avoid being a Losera, you will find traits in her that you can change if they occur in your own self. "If you think you can, you can and if you think you can't, you're right" Mary Kay Ash (Founder of Mary Kay Cosmetics a multi million dollar business).

I say to all aspiring female entrepreneurs, "Snap Out Of It!" Remember when you were a young child and your parents said that you could do anything? They said that you could talk, walk, and ride a bike and so on. If you forgot about this, then do you remember the little engine that could? To succeed in anything, you must revert back to the times when anything was and everything is possible. I feel that one of the most powerful drugs in achieving business success is a strong belief.

The first step to becoming a successful female entrepreneur is to learn to say "NO!" to money conscious poverty and strive for the six figures that you deserve. When we make money, we can hire more people, grow the economy and spread the wealth around.

Here is the profile I've created depicting a successful female entrepreneur whom I call Victoria. She has a happy and positive attitude, in control of her time and stress, eager to try new ideas, takes calculated risks and greets change as an opportunity and not something bad. She feels that life is worth living when you make money. Victoria overlaps her work and play so much that she doesn't know if she is working or playing.

Victoria often thinks of the sweet taste of success as eating her first handful of popcorn. You start and you can't stop until you become successful. The Victorias of the world commonly demonstrate drive, dedication, persistence, diligence and a no-fail entrepreneurial attitude. They are eager to try out new ideas and consider that life is worth living, while becoming a successful entrepreneur. They put their life on fast forward and eagerly look for the next mountain to climb in order to grow their business.

What's the profile of a struggling female entrepreneur that I call Losera? I vision her as one who usually thinks that making money is terrible and that we are snobs when we make money and forget the poor. She feels that she must stay poor and give her profits away. Losera is unhappy most of the time and thinks struggling is part of life and a noble profession. Stress is common, along with bouts of poor health and her life is full of drama, struggles and chaos. Losera hates change and fears new opportunities.

Losera squanders her time on working harder, not smarter. She is set in her ways, has a major fear of failure and is seldom seen as a risk taker. Losera has a high tolerance for low profit margins and underestimates the worth of her product or service. She tends to give away her goods and has an underlying feeling of worthlessness. Asking for more money for her wares is painful and brings guilt because of the fear of rejection. Losera's thoughts are scattered and seldom does she stay focused for any length of time. Many like Losera tend to hold on to the "Hate The Rich" Syndrome because they think that the rich are greedy, insensitive, feel superior and are less caring. Poor is noble and Loseras feel guilty about making money.

Why do some women-owned businesses stay small, while others soar? Loseras have the fear of thinking big, fear competition and feel that real success is not worth the sacrifices. The Loseras of the world that fail in business are usually misfits from the beginning. They are a square peg trying to fit in a round hole. They unconsciously think money is the root of all evil and try to avoid making it at all costs. Loseras avoid success by focusing on the following three areas: *worrying*, *added responsibilities* and *the fear of the unknown*.

Never before have we seen so many women become Victorias, even in business ventures that you would never expect them to enter. According to research by the Spectrem Group, the number of six figure women climbed 68% and only 35% for men from 1996 through 1998.

Now you can discover how to become a Victoria in the business world of tomorrow by implementing these 19 steps today!

Rule 1: Let Go

Let go of the past. Get rid of the memories of former poor employers, former negative friends, former everything that drags you down. Victorias learn from the past, bury it and move on. Most are like a fine racehorse with the main focus of winning the race.

Rule 2: Walk The Part Of A Victoria

Your inner image and outer image must radiate success. Remember that first impression is the only impression. Walk, talk and dress the part of success. Display an "aura" of leadership and refrain from becoming a follower. Add some happiness to everyday life and it will happen if you feel it will.

Rule 3: Go Public

Tell yourself over and over again that you are going to make money, tell the world and eventually, you will. Remember when business gets complicated that's when you run into trouble. Victorias keep their businesses simple and play by the basic rule that more money must come in than what goes out. Don't announce your business idea until you are ready to launch it. This is so a competitor can't steal your idea and beat you to the punch.

Rule 4: Set The Right Goals & Achieve Them

Goals are merely wishes put to writing. Goals need specific objectives that can be readily measured to determine if you have met them. Approximately, 90% of Victorias list their goals, go on to match their goals with measurable objectives and then get ready to act.

Rule 5: Go Into Action & Move

Victorias add the action needed to successfully achieve their goals and objectives. Approximately, 30% of all aspiring female entrepreneurs end up getting into the action stage and finally becoming Victorias. Drive and action are not the same. Victorias move from drive to action, while Loseras spin their wheels in drive and go no place in particular.

Rule 6: Education & Knowledge

Never stop learning. Success comes by staying alert in the lifelong informational arena. Knowledge is the everyday networking that you must do to stay abreast with what is going on in the world.

Rule 7: Play The Part & Believe
Shakespeare could have lived today with his theory that: "All the world's a stage and all the men and women merely players." Victorias radiate success and say over and over again, everyday, that I am a success. She tells others, "I'm good at this and that, this is what I can do for you, this is what I'm worth and I can do anything." Victorias also say, "I'm already a success in my own world and I believe it!"

Rule 8: Make Listening Your Priority
Victorias dominate listening while Loseras dominate talking. You should become a sponge soaking up knowledge no matter what it pertains to. Someday, you may need this information to make an educated decision.

Rule 9: Health Is All In Your Mind
Victorias read their body. After twelve years of dealing with all of the Victorias, I highly recommend that you do everything in moderation such as eating, drinking, exercising and daydreaming. There is a saying that hard work never killed anyone. I think this is true because research reveals that more people become ill from stress than any other reason. Energy, vigor and drive is often found in the content and hard working Victorias may be found working many hours because they don't know the difference between work and recreation, because they seem so much alike. The fun of pursuing and achieving success! Sometimes the Victorias wonder what the next mountain will be that they can climb.

Rule 10: Raise The Bar
Victorias are constantly raising the bar higher and higher and reaching for more. When they stretch their limits, they begin thinking out of the box for other ways to achieve whatever they want. Many Victorias read books on creativity and learn new and innovative strategies to succeed. Loseras tend to moan and groan and blame others for not achieving something. Most Victorias tend to delegate and never do anything that someone else can do for them. They continuously automate and educate on the long-term basis. Going beyond their vision, great entrepreneurs have a strong desire to create something new and introduce things that they think the present world lacks. Victorias look at the world with a sense of wonderment and visualize what it will be like to create something new. They concentrate on outcomes and ignore the obstacles along the way. They have the ability to inspire others by their strong beliefs and total involvement in achieving their vision. Victorias make things happen by getting others excited.

Rule 11: Grow and Become A Contingency Planner
Victorias anticipate that when you plan a project or start-up your own business, something always goes wrong and you better act fast by planning ahead. They

think out of the box and are better equipped to handle problems. I heard Victorias say that if she is not bleeding to death and if she is still breathing, then this is not a true and serious deadline. Victorias seem to think that deadlines are for the dead and not for the living.

Rule 12: Think Money Is Success

Is money the root of all evil? Loseras always go back to this, questioning their state of profitability. Fear of making money is the core to Loseras thinking. Victorias know that money is, in fact, a sign of success and they go all the way to make it. Focus on the profit margin, always keeping it in sight. Their business success is measured by profits. Victorias have one simple rule for their success: "More money must come in than goes out." Victorias keep the operation of their business simple and uncomplicated so that they can make changes swiftly. Not all Victorias have financial skills and they know this so they seek out and use financial advisors. Victorias often hire those who have specific expertise that they don't have. Victorias know that money is not made by chance but by making it their prime purpose. They have a habit of thinking big with workable strategies and with no meaningless efforts. They are women of the future who dare to dream. Their imagination and creativity are fires that light up and fuel their whole business world. Like Onassis, these women succeed by discovering something that their customers can't live without. Recently, a Victoria said to me that customers are friends she has yet to meet. Throughout this text I have highlighted the differences between Victorias and Loseras and the impact of their traits in the success or failure of their business venture.

Rule 13: An Eye For Opportunity

Victorias think out of the box, identify a need and immediately start planning to fill that need. Victorias see things that others don't and are usually calculated risk takers. Victorias are like fine athletes who visualize the trophy before they ever start the race.

Rule 14: Independence

Victorias tend to make quick decisions that they calculate well. When push comes to shove they can take immediately take action on making a decision. They realize that making no decision at all is not the way to run a business. The bottom line for Victorias is to consult with their team, do some additional research and make a timely decision. A team approach may work most of the time, but Victoria knows that she is the company's leader and when it comes to money and taking risk, she must take the lead and make the final timely decisions. Victorias have the ability to think on their feet and make wise decisions.

Rule 15: An Appetite For Systematic Planning

Victorias thrive on hard work, but their ultimate goal is to work smarter not harder. Initially, Victorias will be at the helm working long hours, but very early on you will see them delegating anything that others can do for them. They separate the mundane activities from the things that can make their business venture grow. Victoria, like a racehorse, stays focused bent on winning.

Rule 16: Accept Changes As New Opportunities

There is no other time where changes are common than when you start-up and run your own business. Victorias look at change as times to seize the opportunity to make their business venture even better. A customers' needs and desires change and if you don't realize this early on, then your business is usually doomed for failure. Victorias see changes as opportunities that they have been seeking all along.

Rule 17: Make Stress Work For You

Victorias never sweat the small stuff and most stressful situations are small stuff in their eyes. If the business operation is not bleeding profusely (losing money) and is breathing (still able to make money), then anything is possible. They have the unique skill of being able to sort the small stuff from what really counts in making money.

Rule 18: Making Time Work For You

Victorias know that time is money. When they first start their business, they tend to calculate everything that they do in terms of making money. Loseras waste their time in endless ways such as taking frequent, long and expensive lunches with friends, never getting down to business, never doing their "To Do List" for the day and or week, lack of time to do their strategic planning and pursuing numerous other ways that sabotage their time. Victorias always plan their work and work their plan.

Rule 19: Accept Discipline As A Freedom

Victorias are well aware that as leaders they have a great deal of freedom with time and money and no one to answer to. Victorias use self-discipline to get things done more effectively and efficiently, thereby freeing themselves up for those things important to their success.

After embracing these rules, it is time to focus on your own image. The simplest things can project a certain image, even the tone of your voice. It seems as though people can sense what's going on in your mind just by the tone of your voice. Remember the last time you answered the telephone when you were angry and someone on the other end asked you what was wrong.

When I wake up in the morning, I always look into the mirror and say wow! You look and feel great! After saying this five times, I've convinced myself that I am looking and feeling great, no matter what. Many times, I thank the Author of Life up there for giving me my success and such a great outlook on life. The following are ways to gain a successful attitude:

- Get rid of your fears and gain confidence by practicing like an actor does, remember that all the world's a stage.
- Believe in yourself and your business venture.
- Associate with people who think "winning".
- Be master of your ship and take charge.
- Practice inner thoughts everyday by saying: "I think I can be successful, I know that I can be successful, I will be successful".
- I know that I am the only one who can make me fail and I won't!
- Everyday, write down a negative thought and replace it with a positive one.

Inner image is all in your mind and you can control whether it's good or bad. Most importantly, remember, Victorias have an unshakable belief that they will succeed. One skill that Victorias hold dearly is the power of effective listening. Victorias monopolize listening and Loseras monopolize talking. Victorias use their ears as intake valves. They take a problem, ask others for ideas to solving the problem and then listen for decision-making raw materials. Only then do they take action on their problem. Victorias are the decision-making machines!

Victorias have a 100% work capacity and feed this by being receptive to new ideas and values, soaking up new beliefs and exposing themselves to new viewpoints. They consider themselves forward and progressive thinkers, yet they maintain a streak of kindness.

Loseras have a great deal of difficulty listening and when they do, little is really ever heard. Their destructive attitude closes the door to creative thinking and all that they think about is their impending failure. If you think that you will fail and say that you will fail, then you will fail.

In my twelve years as a mentor, I can't recall hearing a Victoria say that she would fail; it is not in her vocabulary. One Victoria said that she had never thought about failure and asked me if I thought that she was real dumb or real smart. My reply was that her belief of success was so strong, that failure wasn't feasible. This brings us to the power of belief. When you strongly believe something can be done, you tell others that it can be done, and then you usually can find ways to get it done. Believing there is a solution leads the way to getting it done.

I recommend eliminating the following phrases from your vocabulary: *I can't do*, *it won't work*, *don't bother trying* and *it's impossible*. When there is a problem, Victorias often take this negative situation and turn it into some positive phrase. "I don't have enough money," and they change to, "I'm going to make money." The negative is quickly changed into a positive statement that demands action. The action requires brainstorming about how to make more money and sets the mode of positive rethinking.

Along with the planning process goes productive prioritizing for Victorias. They wear many hats both in their personal life and in the business world. Victorias take control by eliminating procrastination, poor planning and personal disorganization. They eliminate time wasters, effectively delegating and building an acceptable level of flexibility into their life. They know where their current time is spent, what their prime time is and recognize how to prioritize.

Victorias routinely create their daily "To Do List" and then prioritize the tasks. Priorities involve what has to be done, should be done and what could be done if some time is left over. Each priority is rated as to its importance and is given a time-frame for completion. Victorias tend to stick to this method until their priorities are completed.

Let go of the past. Victorias learn from the past, bury it and move on. Why is it that some female entrepreneurs soar like eagles (Victorias) and others (Loseras) can barely make it? The business world is full of success stories where thousands of women, no different from you, are getting extraordinary things done. This can be you! There are many entrepreneurial traits that distinguish Victorias from Loseras. Take the time to learn the basic practices that can take you from ordinary to extraordinary.

Be a human Victoria everywhere you go in the business world and radiate honesty, hard work and good character. There are and always will be a few entrepreneurs who lie and cheat to get ahead, only to find themselves in a web of deceit that they can't get out of. It doesn't take long for your customers and employees to learn about dishonest business practices and the word spreads.

I've come to classify women into two categories: takers and givers. The takers are also users. They will get what they want from someone, be it information, assistance or anything else that will help them get ahead. Once they suck the information out of their unaware victim, they then move on to the next victim. Throughout my career, I've met many takers. I guess it's because I'm quite trusting, but I do know that takers only go so far before they fall to the bottom and it's just a matter of time.

I've seen through the years that the givers tend to reap far more than what they give. When you are a giver you must make the distinction between helping someone or having them become reliant on you. You can't let someone become dependent on you, nor can you become their long-term caretaker. There is a fine line between giving to others and sacrificing your own survival and success.

You are a role model for your employees whether you like it or not. If an employee sees you lying to and cheating the customers, they wonder why can't they do it? You must be clear about your business values and beliefs and become a true human model. You will lose other's respect and commitment if you do not. Lead by setting a good example, it may seem simple, but it's the simple rules that will make you a giant in the world of business. Victorias tend to empower their support team because they know that they can't do it by themselves. Many times empowered team players use their strengths to overcome your weaknesses and your whole business soars.

Victorias think they will succeed and they do. Victorias tend to be the cheerleader for their team and realize that the harder it is to accomplish a goal, the sweeter it is when they achieve it.

How many times have you heard someone say, "That person has a personality style all of her own." Don't you often wonder what they mean by this, well I have. Through the years of meeting with thousands of different women, I have developed my own beliefs about personality styles that women assume and how they impact their success or failure. While we can't change our personalities totally, we can play on our strengths and try to avoid the weaknesses associated with each personality type. After describing each personality type, I will mention the advantages for business each offers and point out cautions for business success each personality type should notice. I have developed the following six profiles:

1. The Creative Visionary

Along with your public image there are inner actions that I've come to label, personality styles. One of these styles is the creative visionary who combines a mixture of creative acts, occurring at any given time and place. For a semester at State University of New York at Buffalo, I conducted research on whether or not creative visionaries were born or made. This thesis revealed that many creative visionaries such as artists and poets are, in fact, born creative and yet there is always the other group of individuals who become creative visionaries by cultivating the creative skills that they may not already possess. Of all the skills that positively impact the success of any business, it is the traits and actions of a creative visionary. Through the years of interacting with women who are aspiring to succeed in business, there are many traits that were identified which were causal to their success and being a creative visionary was among the highest. However, this style has to be combined with one of the other personality styles that can add some degree of structure to their actions. I will discuss this in detail later on. I discovered long ago that the creative focus appears to take place at three different levels of thinking:

1. A time of imagery or daydreaming (a successful business image)
2. Illumination (the light bulb goes on)
3. Imagination (searching for skills to make this come to fruition)

After all this, the ideas begin to flow and women like Victorias take action. They never seem to lose their positive and upbeat thinking power, no matter how rough it gets. I also think that creative thinking by visionaries spans four stages:

1. They do their research until it is impossible to go any further.
2. They allow the information to sink into their inner mind by allowing an incubation period.
3. They usually experienced a sudden and exciting period when unexpected ideas and solutions seem to burst through.
4. Their commitment to action causes their creativity to "kick in".

Some Victorias are born with creative skills and other Victorias strive to cultivate these as they go along. I would highly recommend that all women read books on the creative process, participate in creative seminars or training programs and try to start thinking "out of the box", with a sense of positive attitude and wonderment. Victorias generally say that anything is possible and Loseras say that it really won't work. Victorias believe that something can be done and it paves the way for creative solutions. Believing something can't be done is destructive thinking and characteristic of most Loseras. They are usually traditional thinkers and often predict their own failure. If I could cite one difference between Victorias and Loseras, it would be the use of creativity in the planning process. Creative visionaries like Victorias discover new and improved ways of doing almost everything in their pursuit of the "magic blend" of creating a new business. Many Victorias tend to create visual pictures when starting their BAP (Business Action Plan). They actually dream and visualize every aspect of their successful business. Victorias stretch their minds and associate with people in different occupations and social interests so that new ideas are forthcoming. Victorias tend to be original in their ideas, multi-sided in their thinking, versatile; have a sense of wonderment and an ongoing belief that anything is possible. When I talk to Victorias who have succeeded, they tell me that they seem to see things differently than others. They are constantly motivated by the excitement of creating something and nothing "gets them down." It is thought that there are attitudes and conditions for fostering creative minds. One is a time of isolation without exterior stimulations so that you can think about what your business is going to be. This doesn't mean a complete withdrawal, but only a few hours of solitude to prepare for a period of creativity. Daydreaming is often frowned upon in our society, but used by many Victorias. This is a mental activity that is very useful as a promoter of other mental activities and useful in starting the thinking process for going into business. Victorias are commonly free thinkers and are constantly in a state of readiness for latching on to new opportunities and launching new products and/or services. I've observed that the few Victorias who do lack the creativity power find someone to help them with their creativity initiatives. I want to go on record here saying that the majority of all the successful Victorias I've encountered appear to possess a healthy degree of this personality style. Once the creative visionaries do go into business, their continuing creative skills spur them on to invent new goods, reinvent the old goods, think out of the box and expand in ways they never dreamed of or could image. In order to harness some of the creativity, a degree of structure must be added. If all you do is dream and create and there is no action, then how will your business get "off the ground"? This is where another personality style, usually the serious thinker, kicks in to add some structure.

2. The Serious Thinker

A personality style that I have a little trouble dealing with is the serious thinker. Perhaps, it's because I'm a go-getter and a creative visionary. Earlier on, I had to cultivate this serious style within me to add structure to my business venture. Old habits are hard to break but frequently, I have to slow down and do some serious thinking for the health of my business. The pure bred serious thinker is just what it states, they calculate everything, do constant "heavy" thinking, research every single aspect of opening a business to the point that it's impossible to go any further because you have entered the next century. The positive side of the serious thinker is that they are well structured, logical, detailed, conservative, precise, and meticulous and see financial problems, issues and concerns that others don't. They are excellent at financial record keeping and getting the whole job done. The negative side is that they are too rigid, over explaining and impersonal. It's best to keep them away from customers and the incoming calls. They thoroughly read and maintain all memos, business and office literature and their files are overflowing because they have everything ever written on the business. They are at their best when they are performing the financial aspect of a business and are content to be left alone with their calculator. One of your most valuable team players is your financial manager who helps guide you in the most important area of operations. These players are the key to keeping your business financially sound. The area where most businesses get into trouble is financial management and cash flow. It will help if you learn some of their critical thinking skills, so that you become well rounded in every aspect of planning, organizing, implementing and operating your business. Serious thinkers tend to take an enormous amount of time to make decisions. This is acceptable most of the time, but when there are time-sensitive decisions that have to be made to successfully operate your business, they sometimes "miss the boat." I recall one example of a serious thinker who wanted to open a Computer Repair Center. She had it all... technical skills; her completed Business Action Plan, years of experience, waiting customers, all of the technical equipment and a great location in a busy strip mall. The dilemma here was that she researched this business opportunity to death and someone else coup the lease on her site and opened this type of business. I strongly recommend that you include the serious thinker in all meetings that deal with cash flow, all money matters, major changes that impact the bottom line, delinquent accounts, the purchase of major furnishing or equipment and any other areas that could impact growth. It would bode well if you aren't a serious thinker to bring this person into your operation and learn from them.

3. The Crowd Pleaser

Some of the most pleasant women that I know have a crowd pleaser personality. They are warm and pleasant, usually dress casual, belong to most of the local clubs and are always delighted to see you and ready to chat. Most of my best friends have this personality and I guess that we are friends because they make me feel good when I'm around them. Crowd pleasers take people's feeling into consideration, are excellent at public relations and dealing with all types of customers. People love them and they thrive on the attention they give. Sometimes they let their work slip because of their unending socialization. They are the morale builders in a company and can remain pleasing even under unpleasant circumstances. The downside of this personality style is that they are usually overly sensitive and thought of as being too soft when tough behavior is required. I think that this person is best at handling customers and not in high power decision-making roles. One thing that you have to remember with this style is that they have to be harnessed because of their tendency to chat, roam to meet others and forget that lunch is only an hour.

4. The Live Wire

Here is my favorite kind of personality style because I have always been one since an early age. When I was nine, I played the violin in school recitals and didn't like the songs the teacher selected, so I wrote my own. She commended me, but later she told my mother that I was not a team player in the orchestra. In college, both at the undergraduate and graduate levels, I drove myself to achieve A's in almost every course. I was relentless at this and now when I look back, I see how silly this was, because no one has ever asked me what my marks were. I've change my way of thinking a great deal since then and have learned to balance work and play. The live wire often says, "Getting the job done is what I do best". They are found optimizing profits and being up-to-date on all of the latest business trends that impact the business. This is the person that you want and need to keep you abreast with the achieving goals and outcomes and assisting you to set the bar even higher. The negative side of this personality is that they are often insensitive to other people's feelings, too abrupt in their approach to everybody and like taking command, rather becoming a team player. It is essential to include the live wire on your management team to keep the business high rolling, growing and prosperous. No other member will be more dedicated in the quest to excel and make money.

5. The Leader

The leader personality is one who demonstrates high performance, innovative thinking and aligns herself with futuristic movements. Leaders are inclined to read and know about all the other great leaders past, present and potential future. They realize that information is power in the business arena and put what they have learned into practice at every opportunity by always raising the bar. Leaders see excitement in risk taking and view demands made upon them as legitimate burdens as part of being the leader. Handling the stress brought on by multiple changes, leaves the leader excited and in a state of anticipation. They see changes as grand opportunities waiting to happen. I believe that effective leaders make decisions rapidly and changes slowly and let no one put them down. Leaders seem to feel it's urgent and essential that they identify and address their emerging fears and move on. They free their minds of worry and reduce the reality of the fear factor by comprehensive planning that includes written goals, objectives, performance outcomes and a monitoring and evaluation system. One of the negative leadership aspects is that sometimes they are so independent that they forget to be one of the team players. Leaders also tend to feel that others around them should be as capable as them and sometimes they have difficulty with those around them who are slow at decision-making.

6. The Follower

I named this personality because it is the complete opposite of the leader. She hangs back most of the time, dislikes making decisions and is seldom an independent thinker. Now I'm not saying that the follower is not likeable, only that she gets lost in the crowd and her business takes a "back seat" in her life. Most followers go about their everyday living saying to themselves; "If I don't make a decision, then I won't be wrong." Many of them perform what is expected but little more. They are usually stress free and completely at ease with those around them because they let someone else handle responsibilities. I've not encountered too many independent followers who have ever completed their Business Action Plan and few who have gone on to start their business. The one exception is the followers who become partners. In these cases, the other partner is the leader who makes all of the decisions, leads the team and performs around them. Recently, I had the opportunity to meet with two partners. After an hour of discussion about their upcoming business expansion, I noted that the follower never made one remark or offered any input into the conversation. Eventually, I realized that the follower was the investor and the leader was very happy to lead the project.

I would like to summarize the six personality styles by saying that you should examine your own style and determine which one, two or three that you are. Initially, every woman will fall into the leader or the follower style. Then as you go on to explore your other specific characteristics, you will discover that you will also fit into some of the remaining categories. The more characteristics that you have in each of the categories, the more you will bring to your business venture.

Currently, I fall into three categories: the leader, live wire and crowd pleaser. I have few traits of the creative visionary and even fewer as a critical thinker. However, I am working on becoming more creative by reading and practicing the levels of creative thinking. I don't think I will ever be a critical thinker, but I had enough vision to recognize this early on.

Before I started my first business, I realized that my financial experience and expertise were very limited and that my business could suffer because of this. Before I launched my business, I solved the problem by hiring one of most gifted financial managers around. I knew her value and in the first few years, she made a higher salary than I. A decade later she is still with my company, helping to grow my four businesses beyond my wildest dreams!

Perhaps, you find categorizing personalities into styles is a little unusual, but I found that it is one means of discovering what people around you are made of and what turns them on to making them produce (or not produce). I will leave you with one thought: you probably won't like a person who is the opposite of your personality, but each style brings with it new and different strategies that can help make or break your business. Before you even start your business, read over this chapter and make certain that all of the personality styles are part of your team. If you have many of these traits yourself, bravo, but if you do not you need to compensate for this lack. Early on, I realized that my financial experience and expertise were lacking and that my business could suffer from this shortcoming. However, it was all right because I proceeded to hire a financial expert.

Another important aspect to projecting a better image is to work on your speaking style. I highly recommend that women lower their voices at least an octave or two because we tend to raise our voice when we get excited or when we are speaking in front of people. You may want to record yourself speaking at home and then play it back for your review. The following are suggestions to help you develop your speaking style:

- Make certain that everyone can hear you at your presentations.
- Avoid rambling, stuttering or reading every word when you present.
- Watch humor and slang.
- Pilot test your speech on family and friends.
- Use props to add dimension and impact, if appropriate.
- All of your handouts, brochures, catalogs, cards etc. should be top quality.

Your speaking style should radiate expertise, honesty, a high level of energy, listening power, effective communications skills and positive body language. Let's discuss body language and what this really means. Through the years, researchers have professed that if you stand up tall, it radiates self-confidence, if you look people straight in the eyes, then you are honest and the list goes on and on. May I recommend that you read a text on body language and give some of the suggestions a try. What have you got to lose?

One of the characteristics of Victorias that I feel is important to expanding your customer base is the ability to recall customers' names and something special about each customer. I have asked many Victorias their secret and this is what I discovered along the way.

Have you ever met a new customer of two months, only to go blank when trying to remember her name when you meet her again? You begin to talk, hoping it will come to you. The longer you talk without using her name, the more she suspects that you don't know it. She may think that you are not a very good businessperson because of your lack of memory. The next time you want to do business with her she may not want to remember your name. That is a customer lost!

Victorias tend to agree that customers want to feel special and important. Now that you know the importance of memory skills, we will discuss how to get your memory working better. Our brain absorbs and stores information for us to recall later on when we need it. The problem is that we have to pay attention in order to deposit information that we can recall in the future.

You have heard the saying "In one ear and out the other." Most of the time it is difficult to pay attention when someone lacks something unique, exciting or special. Memory retention requires the learning of paying attention to the little details.

Mental imagery is one of the learning skills that work quite well for increasing memory retention. Let's suppose you meet a new customer named Mara Green. Immediately, you need to select something unique to remember about this customer and then commit it to memory. She may resemble your Aunt Mara who is very fond of green. Say her name over three times while thinking to yourself that she does look like your aunt. Use her name at least three times in the initial conversation, while concentrating on this association. You must hear the name aloud to have it stored for later use. It will now allow this connection to sink deeper into your memory for recall when you meet her again.

Another Victoria once told me she takes the name of new customers and associates them with her favorite actors or actresses. She met a new customer named Annie and immediately associated her with the actress in the stage play Annie. She finds something that they both have in common such as red hair and this becomes an easy way of remembering her customer's name. Victorias remember that when their memory is sharp it appears that they are well-informed businesswomen. Besides, it's nice not to have the stress of being unable to recall a customer's name.

Have you ever heard that the first impression is the only impression? Well, take it from me it is true! This chapter covers the art of super selling. Our image must reflect positive qualities in order to become a super seller of your business. Over the years, I have come to realize just how important it is to sell yourself and your business.

One of the factors that I constantly evaluate when I'm performing and conducting workshops is the impact of my outer image. I have performed for years before audiences of all sizes and have seldom received a poor or average post evaluation. This is not by accident, but by my persistence in creating an exceptional outer image. My post evaluations are critical to documenting my success and ultimately these assessments impact my profits.

I do everything I can to get my customers to contract with me again and outstanding evaluations are the mechanism. I always wear light colors when I perform or meet with my customers because years ago I read that light colors radiate honesty, purity and trust. Now whether this is true or not, I've abided by this rule over the past decade. Once I tested the truth of this theory by performing in a black pin stripe suit at one of my workshops. It was a disaster from the onset! Initially, I thought this was just a coincidence and so a month later I repeated wearing the black pin stripe suit. Once again, this workshop was rated below my usual high ratings. The suit went into the Good Will collection the very next day. Say what you like, but I wasn't going to test this theory anymore and to this day I wear only light colored suits when I perform or go to meet my customers.

I will share a little humor with you here. When I conducted earlier workshops, I wore reading glasses. I had to put them on to read my handouts and take them off to see the audience. The participants in several workshops began to state on the post evaluation that this annoyed them. My staff was very upset (maybe it's because they sort of like me) and said that the participants were cruel and mean. Now I teach that the purpose of post evaluations are to give you feed back and I took these remarks seriously. I went to the eye doctor, got fitted for contacts and that ended the negative post evaluation remarks. The lesson here is that your outer image can impact your customers' ratings of you. Therefore, you should do everything you can to enhance your outer appearance.

Other hints on outer image include the following:
- Pay attention to caring for your hair, nails, dress and shoes.
- Shower or bathe daily and use perfume sparingly.
- Discover the best way to use and wear your make up.
- Keep abreast with new hairstyles and try one.
- Sit tall, walk and stand erect.
- Watch your body language.
- Every morning and evening ask yourself, "Would I buy from me".

Make certain that when people view your outer image, they see you as successful. One bad habit I had was putting my hands in my pockets when I met my customers and many etiquette authors consider this as a negative sign. My staff quickly solves this problem by sewing up all of my pockets. I accepted this with some pain, but I will do anything I can to enhance my chances with customers.

I strongly recommend that you get excited about what you are selling, believe in it and become an expert in your field. Then you can start to write for the news media about your product, service or your specific expertise. I say to you that if you can talk, then you can write, it's as simple as that! I propose that you try to write a short article and soon it will become second nature to you. Then you can send one to the local newspaper. The editor will be thrilled to receive it because they are always looking for something to fill the many columns before the paper goes to print.

I began writing editorials and news articles over ten years ago about how to start a business, effective communications, stress and time management and a variety of other topics that I thought the readers would like. I insisted that my photo be published with all my articles because a picture is worth a thousand words. You too must insist that your photo be included at all times. My articles are still being published after all these years and sometimes I find it difficult to keep up. So why do I write these articles when I don't get paid? The rationale is that it keeps my picture and name out in the public and frequently new customers come my way because of my name and pictures.

- You must be able to think on your feet.
- Speak about your business at a moment's notice.
- Practice, practice, practice what you are going to speak about.
- Learn all that you can about your buyers.
- Learn to state the rewards for buying from you.
- Volunteer to speak anywhere and everywhere about your business.

You must know everything there is about your product or service by reading, contacting the experts, listening, finding a mentor in the same field and believing in what you are doing. With this knowledge, it will generate ongoing confidence.

As a woman entering the world of entrepreneurship, you are going to be a part of the gigantic wave that's growing in size and sweeping across America. Many business researchers predict that in the future, approximately 60% of all new innovations and changes will come from women like you and me in the business arena throughout our nation and the world.

While numerous major businesses and Fortune 500 companies are closing their doors, downsizing and becoming lean and mean, thousands of new women businesses are emerging. In the year two thousand ten, it is projected that approximately eighty-five per cent of all working people will be employed by small businesses and women will own half of these businesses (United States Department of Labor, 2002).

Many like yourself feel lost in the wilderness of going into business, not realizing that advice and support are available to you. All that you need to know is what there is readily available and where to look. There are Entrepreneur Centers and Women's Business Centers like ours, libraries, business workshops and seminars that can get you started in your business planning, but there is no author like I, as candid and full of hints as I reveal in this text.

CHAPTER TWO
Starting Your Business

After you have inventoried your own strengths and weaknesses as a businesswoman and decided that you either are or can become a Victoria, you are ready to prepare to start your business. Loseras often rush into a business without proper planning. Victorias plan such issues as what kind of business they are going to enter, what kind of customers they will be appealing to, the location of their prospective business, and what assistance they will need. Victorias take the time and effort to think through and articulate the issues involved in starting up and running a business venture. Articulating and organizing your thoughts will become your Business Action Plan (BAP).

You may be thinking, "Why should I take the time to create my Business Action Plan?" The benefit is that it is your path to follow to make money because it guides you through the turbulent economic seas and into a harbor of choice. Your BAP is your business profile and allows you an official document to take to your lenders or anyone else who may need to know about your operation. When others read your BAP, it gives them a silhouette of your anticipated business and lends credibility on whether or not your venture will be successful.

The BAP is your communication tool when you need to orient such people as your employees, sales personnel, and suppliers, about your operations. This plan portrays you as a strong and focused business leader and manager. It can give you practice in thinking about such issues as competitive conditions, opportunities, threats, and cash flow. Such wrestling with issues can make you a giant in the business world of tomorrow.

The entire Business Action Plan is aimed at making profits. I sense that successful women feel responsible for their own money, depend on no one else to pay their bills, and believe that money buys power in the business arena.

In order to succeed you need to consider the following questions and more: What business am I going into? What product or service will I offer? Where are my customers? How much money do I need to get started? How much money will I charge? These are only a few of the questions that are addressed in this text. You may be thinking, "Why should I waste my time on drawing up a plan?" The benefits of a BAP are endless! It provides a path to follow to generate profits. It is also your business profile to give to bankers, as well as a communication tool. But most of all, it is your road map to success.

If you are thinking of going into business, you should initially examine the pros and cons of starting this specific business venture. Ask yourself these questions to determine if this business venture is for you: Is there a sufficient number of customers and will it be profitable? Such thinking is easy to do. Draw a line down a sheet of paper with pros on one side and cons on the other. Find some quiet time to examine your options.

Along with the pros and cons of starting your business, ask yourself the following twelve questions to determine if going into business is for you:
1. Do I have the skills and expertise to start this type of business?
2. Have I located some customers?
3. Am I an exceptional leader and manager?
4. Can I handle stress?
5. Do I manage my time well?
6. Do I have a strong and unfailing belief that I will succeed?
7. Am I self-disciplined in order to get things done?
8. Am I really success oriented?
9. Can I handle changes?
10. Do I have the financial skills?
11. Am I a hard worker and result oriented in my thinking?
12. Do I have some special talents that will help me in this business?

The more yes responses to these questions, the more likely you are to become successful. This is nothing more than taking a look at the entrepreneurial world that you want to enter and identifying your internal strengths and weaknesses. Start by examining your strengths: do you have what it takes to start this business and do you have the expertise and educational background needed to succeed? What are your weaknesses, and how will you address these?

You should also identify your external opportunities and challenges that you may have been unaware of before now. Once you have decided that the pros outweigh the cons, you are ready to proceed to your next planning initiative.

Approximately, 95% of all the Victorias I've met go on to create a strong Business Action Plan. My records reveal that about 75% of all Loseras who start their BAP never complete it. Procrastination, the inability to seek help, and the lack of focus hinder Loseras from ever completing their BAP.

Loseras usually see no value in writing a purpose statement and they frequently skip over this. On the other hand, Victorias demand a precise purpose statement for their business and won't budge until it is clearly written.

Point 1 of the BAP: Establishing the Purpose and Nature of the Business
The first step in creating your BAP can be taken once you have researched whether or not there are sufficient customers to generate profits. The BAP involves developing eight points. The how to will be addressed throughout this text. Your plan begins with a clear and concise purpose statement of the business that you are going to start. This statement reflects what your business is really all about.

I have developed the following eight questions to help you develop your purpose statement:

1. What business am I really starting?
This may sound like a silly question, yet many businesses go broke because of the confusion about what business they are really in. Victoria researches and develops her BAP before she launches her business. Losera tends to start her business without planning or research.

2. What is the name of my business going to be?
Your business name should reflect something related to your business venture and not just a series of initials. Victoria tries to add meaning to her business name. One Victoria started a cleaning business with the name "*Handy Woman.*"

3. What will my business image be, and what makes my business unique?
Your image should reflect what you are selling that is unique. Remember that if there is nothing unique about your products or services, then don't start the business. Victoria knows that the uniqueness of her business is the reason for launching her business. In addition, she is aware that the first impression is the most important impression. Both the interior and exterior of your business should reflect beauty.

4. When will my grand opening take place?
This is the time when you launch your business, announcing to the world that you're out there. Victoria spends additional advertisement dollars at this time. Losera does nothing more than wish that customers would come to her opening.

5. What hours will I be open?
Conduct a brief survey early on asking your potential customers what hours they would like your business to be open. These hours can be adjusted later on when you identify your customers' choice of hours.

6. What initial inventory will I need, and is there enough money for buying the inventory?
You should calculate how much inventory you will initially need. If you need more, you must discover if it can be quickly procured. Your initial start-up must include ample inventory.

7. Is my business impacted by seasonal fluctuation?
You have to pay fixed monthly expenses all year long. If there is a downturn, your profit margin suffers. I would recommend considering eBay as one strategy in coping with the seasonal times.

8. How can I calculate if and when my business will generate a profit?
Will enough of my customers be able to afford my products or services? I recommend stopping right here when you see no hope of profits in this business venture. Losera will just continue her fragmented planning and head for disaster.

After articulating the purpose statement for your business, the next step is to contact an attorney. Before you go into business, take the time to interview several attorneys in order to decide on which one suits your needs. If after an interview your gut feeling is that you are not going to be compatible, then move on to another, until you find one that can guide you with their legal expertise. In addition, I recommend that you never sign a legal document of any type until your attorney reads and approves it.

You should consult your attorney immediately for assistance in selecting the legal form that best suits your individual business. You must decide up front what legal business form your company will assume. The following explains some types of legal business forms:

Sole Proprietorship
Once you have a purpose statement, then you must decide on what legal form your business will assume. The sole proprietorship is where many entrepreneurs begin because it is simple to do and costs very little. Since a sole proprietorship means that you have no partners, a lawyer is not needed for your DBA filing. No legal papers are required except a business license called a DBA (Doing Business As) and a name filing with the county clerk. The cost of a DBA is usually less

than $30. You need not file a separate income tax return, because the business is you and you are the business. Business and personal tax returns are filed together. One disadvantage of a DBA is that if you die, then the business dies with you. In addition, you are personally liable for all business debts. Creditors can go after all your assets such as personal property, bank accounts, and your house.

Partnership

I feel that a partnership can be very dangerous because each partner is liable for the other's actions. If one partner skips town, the other is left holding the bag. In any legal action, each partner will be sued for property, bank accounts, etc. The cost of setting up a partnership agreement varies. It is more than a DBA and a little less than establishing a corporation. Since costs vary with attorneys, shop around to find the right lawyer for you at a fee that you can afford. Consult with your attorney about all of the partnership issues that can directly and personally impact you. Don't use your partner's attorney even if her services are free because your partner's attorney is not going to watch out for your welfare. It is my feeling that it is easier to get out of a marriage than a partnership. It is my experience that very few survive the breakup without the collapse of the business. An attorney is a must in setting up the partnership agreement. I recommend that you ask yourself this important question: Why do I need a partner? If it's money you need for your business startup, then why not try a financial institution or venture capitalist? If it's someone to help manage the business that you need, then why not hire a manager and retain full control of your company?

Limited Partnership

There is limited partnership, which is much like a corporation, except that the investors become limited partners. Limited partners are only personally liable for the amount that they have invested. This is a great way to help you start or grow your business without giving up any control.

Incorporation

A safer choice for a business is to become a corporation. This is a state-chartered organization owned by shareholders. The shareholders can elect or appoint a board of directors who are ultimately responsible for the management of the business. When you incorporate, your business exists as a separate entity. The corporate shield personally protects you unless you are grossly negligent or there is fraud. You are an employee of the corporation. If you die or leave, the business can go on. The advantage to incorporating is that financial institutions are more likely to give a loan to a corporation rather than a sole proprietor because they feel that this business shows some structure. One disadvantage of incorporating is that you must hold regular meetings and file an annual report.

Limited Liability Corporation

This is also a state-chartered organization that provides a reduced liability for a corporation, but differs in the tax advantage of a partnership or sub chapter S corporation. Corporation, Subchapter S, and Limited Liability Corporation are all forms that you should discuss with your attorney. The legal costs are about the same for all three of these incorporation forms. Some entrepreneurs feel that they can handle the entire process of incorporation themselves, bypassing the use of an attorney in order to save money. I feel that contracting with an attorney is essential in preventing legal problems later on.

Franchise

Many economists say that franchising is the wave of the future for starting a business. If this is indeed the upcoming strategy for creating a new business, then all those women looking to purchase a franchise should review the guidelines listed here. Franchising is commonly described as an industry or business. It is neither of these; it is a way of doing business. It is marketing a product or service that has already been accepted and used in a wide variety of businesses. Some of the franchise businesses may have only one thing in common - a franchise system of distribution. Other franchises are more complex and may encompass the entire range of the methods of operation. There is no single definition of franchising. The overall definition of a franchise is usually stated in a contract or agreement between the franchisee (the buyer) and the franchiser. A prospective franchisee should always consult an attorney and their accountant to conduct a thorough investigation of a franchise opportunity before investing. The advantage of buying into a franchise system is that it is combining the efforts of an independent businessperson with the experience and skills of a strong partner. In return for the use of the franchise system, the franchiser will require money from the franchisee. The franchiser will also require certain conduct in order to maintain the quality and standards necessary to preserve the franchiser's image and good will. It is well to remember that with the boom of franchising comes the usual quota of unqualified and unsuitable promoters who attempt to pass themselves off as one of the successful franchisers. During the 70's, franchising was often thought of as the fast and easy way to get rich quick. Numerous newspaper articles related vivid stories about the success of franchisees that got in on the ground floor and accumulated untold wealth. Unfortunately, the stories also attracted con artists and those without business ethics who saw franchising as a way to make a fast buck. Soon newspapers were writing about people who were cheated out of their life savings. In response to the growing number of complaints, in 1979 the Federal Trade Commission (FTC) enacted trade regulations that were to govern the amount of information that the franchiser has to disclose to a potential franchisee before the sale could be completed. This information is furnished to a franchisee in the form of a disclosure document. In 1992, to add further controls to the federal regulations of franchising, more demanding regulations requiring a more detailed disclosure than the earlier federal rule, it is called the Uniform Franchise Offering Circular (UFOC). Investigate the company's directors and officers. Some of this information can be found in the disclosure document. Beware of rushing into a franchise investment. The following areas warrant investigation:

- The litigation history of the franchiser is very important and should be thoroughly researched as to any pending lawsuits. If there is one, then this warrants a closer look by your attorney.
- Contact other franchisees because they usually will not hide their complaints.
- Consult your attorney about the initial and continuing costs paid to the franchiser such as franchise fees, training costs, on-site start-up costs, royalties, promotional costs, equipment, supplies, and opening inventory. Some may be initial costs and others may be ongoing.
- Your ability to receive management training and assistance from the franchise team is critical to your success. Investigate the strengths and weaknesses of the franchise management team.
- Learn about the use of the trademarks, service marks, trade names, logos, and copyrights that are the heart of the franchise system.
- Current franchise laws contain specific requirements as to how and when franchisers may furnish sales and profit projections. Many franchisers will not even address this area.
- Franchises are usually granted for the operation at or from a particular site. Seek your attorney's advice as to the legal limitations on the extent to which an exclusive franchise protects you.
- Understand the franchise contract provisions related to operating controls, practices, and assistance. You don't want to create an unhappy relationship because of a misunderstanding about the franchise operations and its practices.
- Usually, a franchise agreement is for ten or twenty years. You may decide that you want to sell or transfer your franchise to your children. Your ability to sell is another critical aspect of your franchise agreement. You should know whether or not you can sell your franchise at the time that you initially purchase it. Some franchisers will want to buy the business back, while others will let you sell it to someone else. It all depends on your initial agreement that you and your attorney agreed upon with the franchiser.

One woman that I mentored had always wanted to own her own pizzeria. Victoria had saved enough money to buy a Pizza Oasis franchise. She had managed a pizzeria for over ten years and learned all about operating the pizza business.

Her greatest fear was that she might have the hands-on experience, but she had very little education beyond high school. When I asked her what she felt that she would have trouble with, she mentioned the finances and bookkeeping. The rest she thought she could handle.

I recommended that she ask the franchiser for advice about this specific issue. He said that when she purchased their franchise, this training was included. If she felt that this area wasn't covered thoroughly enough in the franchise training, then she had two options: research other pizza franchises that included more comprehensive financial training, or seek a CPA firm to handle her finances. Victoria chose to hire a financial manager for her business operation.

The International Franchise Association regularly distributes a brochure about the most commonly asked questions about franchising. If you are truly interested in the franchise system, then by all means obtain this.

A few years ago, two young women who were working in the floral business came in to talk about purchasing the Ace Florist Shop franchise. Lois and Mandy had been friends since college. Ten years later, they wanted to partner in this venture. Lois provided all of the money that was left to her by her grandmother to purchase this franchise. Mandy was going to help manage the shop because it would be open twelve hours a day, seven days a week. I questioned what Mandy's financial investment would be. The reply was that Mandy had no money but was willing to share the long hours. I recommended that Mandy be hired as the manager while Lois retained 100% ownership of this franchise package. After Mandy refused to accept the management position, Lois interviewed and eventually selected a well-qualified person for the manager's job.

After you have decided what form your business should take, you must secure the proper business forms. Initially, your company must assume some type of legal business form. The specific form should be determined in concert with the guidance and advice from your attorney. You may want to seek advantages by being WBE certified. Becoming certified as a Women's Business Enterprise (WBE) could give a woman-owned business visibility.

The basic requirement for WBE certification is that 51% of the business is owned and operated by a woman. This company must provide a useful product or service and not just be a shell or pass-through to another company. A woman has to be in charge and actively work in the business setting. The woman leader must have the time, skills, experience, and confidence to participate in the bidding process.

Sometimes a husband and wife own the business, but the husband puts 51% in his wife's name because of these certification requirements. Another situation is where a wife holds all of the stocks, but her husband controls the everyday operations. Both of these cases will be denied certification because of the lack of control by the women involved here.

Getting WBE certified is not easy, but involves disclosure of extensive financial and personal data, willingness to have an on-site visit by the certifying agent, maintaining a strong cash flow, success in delivering the product or service, and playing a leadership role in the company. To find out more about WBE certification, check out www.sba.gov/sdb or contact Small Business Administration, Office of Business Development at (202) 619-1850.

Many women tend to worry about having their business ideas stolen and it is vital to keep this in mind. I highly recommend that you not reveal to others the details of your business idea, particularly if these people could be your competitors.

If you think that your idea qualifies for legal protection, contact your attorney to discuss the following protection options:
- Copyright: to protect printed materials and/or software.
- Patent: to protect your original device, prototype, or process.
- Trademark: to guard your product's name, logo, symbol, or figure.
- Service mark: to guard a brand or service name, logo, symbol, or figure.

The following are six basic steps to ensure sufficient legal protection:
1. If sharing information, record the date and the name of the person with whom you shared it.
2. Be aware of the character of every person with whom you discuss your idea and BAP.
3. Request that those who view your BAP sign a nondisclosure agreement.
4. Request employees sign a non-competition agreement.
5. File for your copyright, patent, trademark, or service mark early on.
6. To protect your ownership rights, secure the services of an attorney who is experienced in these matters.

For more information on copyright, contact the Copyright Office, Library of Congress, Washington, D.C., 20559; for patents and trademarks log on to www.uspto.gov.

Another important aspect of achieving success in business is your location. Staying home-based has its advantages because it saves you overhead expenses;

however, you should not remain home-based if customers have to come to you to purchase your goods. Proper site is very important to your business success when customer traffic is needed for sales. If customers are coming to your house to purchase products, then you must be zoned to operate a home-based business. It is also important to research whether or not your insurance covers any and all customer liabilities.

A limited number of customers may eagerly purchase products at your home, no matter how obscure your location. However, the majority of customers want a business that is easily accessible in a highly traveled area where other complementary stores are located. This is especially true if your sales are based on impulse buying.

The ideal location outside the home should include ample parking, good signage, sufficient lighting, and safety. Your store should be handicapped accessible, with wide walkways to accommodate a wheelchair.

If you are leasing a site, you may have to do renovation such as painting and adding shelves or counters. You may want or have to do these yourself. Negotiate with the owner to see if you can come to an agreement on who will pay for the renovations if you do them. Many times the owner will credit these costs toward your rent, entirely or partially. It doesn't hurt to ask about this because every dollar that you put into this site will not be recouped when and if you leave. Be certain to ask who does the snow plowing and the outside maintenance and who pays for these services. Inquire if there is a cost for trash removal or any other hidden costs to the lessee.

Before you purchase a sign you must ask questions because many times landlords have specific restrictions on what size and type of signs they will allow. It is a sad Losera who paid hundreds of dollars for a sign only to have it denied by the landlord.

Conrad Hilton, owner of the Hilton hotel chain, stated many times that success in business means location, location, and location. I remember a visit to one store where they sold beautiful clothing for all the family at very reasonable prices. There were few, if any, customers. I knew that this store was in trouble because I had difficulty finding it, there was no parking, and it was on a street that had very few cars going by. I asked the proprietor why she selected this site. She replied, "It's what I could afford." At this point, she was having difficulty even paying the current amount. My recommendations were to find a smaller site in the downtown area with lots of cars and people. She explained her problems to the landlord, who was unaware of her difficulties. He offered her a smaller space at a downtown site that he owned and agreed to help her move. He even agreed upon an acceptable rent for the first year so that she could get started. Within the year, she went on to become the key retail store in the landlord's downtown complex.

If you are fortunate enough to have a business incubator in your area, then by all means take a look at whether or not this site is for you. The purpose of a business incubator is to reduce small business failures by making it easier for them to survive the critical early stages of business development. This is achieved by providing inexpensive space, access to commonly required administrative support services, shared resources, and technical assistance. All new businesses make mistakes, but the incubator gives new companies some breathing room to learn from errors that otherwise could be fatal. In addition, valuable working capital is preserved by the reduced overhead costs at this site. The long-term goal of most incubators is to graduate their tenants into conventional quarters when the business is strong enough to stand on its own.

Remember earlier that I mentioned that I started one of my businesses in a local business incubator and stayed there for the full three years. The incubator provided us with low-cost rent, shared services, management advice, and a group of small business owners to network with. Incubators widely vary among individual economic projects and are usually one of the components of the economic development strategies aimed at creating new businesses and new jobs. Ultimately, economic growth will result.

The success of a new business venture cannot be guaranteed. It is determined by multiple factors that impact the marketplace. However, for many small businesses, the incubator can substantially increase the probability of survival.

Point 2 of the BAP: Determining Customer Potential
Victoria lives by the basic rule that if there are no customers, then there are no profits and there is no way she is going to start this business. She is fully aware that customers are lifelines. She will not accept the failure to find customers as an excuse. Now we will start developing Point 2 of your BAP. This point deals with customers. Initially, we will explore identifying and locating your customers. This is one of the most important elements in your plan, because without sufficient customers, there will be few sales, resulting in insufficient profits.

I often say, "Customers are made of gold, and if you have them you have a gold mine." Here you will research who your customers are, where you will find them, how you can reach them, and what will make them buy from you. Ask yourself

the following questions:
1. Who are your potential customers?
2. Where are they located?
3. Why would customers buy your products or services?
4. Will they pay the amount that you set in order for you to realize a decent profit?

Victoria usually begins thinking about starting her own business because she finds products or services that are not being addressed. A good rule of thumb used by Victoria is to line up sufficient customers before opening the door. The numbers needed to break even will vary according to the product or service, fixed monthly expenses, and any other costs that have to be paid out.

Victoria conducts surveys by selecting random people to ask whether or not they would buy her product, if and when available. It is a sad Losera business that starts without a customer in sight! Many times Losera kicks off her business without having a clue who her customers really are. Losera usually starts a business with a product or service that she likes in hopes that the customers will be found later.

One Losera started a sweet shop selling only chocolate candy products made from family recipes. She never considered that not everyone liked chocolate, and many customers passed her by because they had no other choice. In addition, the family recipes had some expensive ingredients that negatively impacted the profit margin. These sound like simple problems, but unless you have sufficient customers that are willing to buy your products or services at a reasonable price, you will not survive, much less make a profit.

Here is one question I often ask myself: "Is customer service a lost art?" When I look back at the last time I experienced good customer service, it was well over a month ago. It was when I visited one of our recent graduates who opened a used clothing store. She greeted me with a big smile, offered me a cup of tea, and took pride in showing me suits that were my size and in the colors she knew I liked. Why is it that when we do receive excellent customer service it makes such a good impression on us that we usually choose to go back? It's probably because good customer service is a lost art in today's business world. The following are seven tips to help develop great customer service skills:
1. Listen to your customers by being slow to speak and quick to listen.
2. Smile! It is the best way to show that you are happy the customer came.
3. Allow your customer space to browse.
4. Always put the customer in your store first, even above a telephone call.
5. Teach your employees the importance of providing excellent customer service.

6. Handle irate customers sensitively, offering to do anything in order to solve the problem. Remember that the goal is to fix the problem as quickly as possible.
7. Always thank your customer, whether a purchase was made or not.

Here you are in the midst of planning on starting up your business. You've selected an ideal location, located a sufficient customer base, and are working diligently on your *BAP - Points 1 and 2 of your BAP have been developed, and now you are ready to move on.*

Point 3 of the BAP: Initial Start-up Costs

In order to launch a successful business in the eyes of the public, it must radiate success from day one and give the image that it is, indeed, successful! How this is accomplished is through different strategies, depending on whether your business is home-based or located in a busy mall. I profess that your business image is all wrapped up in your packaging. This means that the major visible sign that your company portrays must be one of wealth, prosperity, and unquestionable success. You have to appear that you are flying with the winners.

Initial startup costs are what it takes to set up your business, and it is important to identify these costs and determine whether or not you can afford them. My first office furnishings in the incubator site were those claimed from a business that went bankrupt. Though they were like new, I was able to purchase them at less than fifty per cent of their original value. Additional office pieces were bought from a vendor who had second hand furnishings obtained at auctions. These were also of fine quality, and I saved hundreds of dollars while creating the image of elegance.

Office set up with all furniture should include desks, filing cabinets, chairs, lamps and any other piece of furniture that you add to your office. When you want to purchase new equipment, I recommend getting prices from three separate vendors so that you can compare prices and quality. You may want to consider leasing your equipment if money is tight. Remember to include the maintenance charge, whether you purchase or lease.

Other startup costs include the following:
- Computer hardware and software costs. Some vendors will include computer training at an additional cost.
- Business and office supplies to include business cards, paper, copy paper, pens, paper clips, and anything else needed to kick off your business.
- Telephone system and set up. Find out the initial installation fee that can

sometimes be costly. I remember that when we moved into the hotel site, it cost seven hundred dollars to run the telephone lines to our offices.

- Signage for your business outside and inside so that customers can find you.
- First time deposits for utilities, telephone, and any other fees.
- Legal fees and licenses that you may need.
- Other costs may include an initial accounting charge for setting up your accounting system or the one-time lawyer fee to get you started.
- Some owners include the initial advertisement costs, because it is a one time, higher than usual amount.

Aside from the startup costs, you must account for the following fixed monthly expenses:

- Rent or lease costs.
- Utilities, if they are not included in your lease.
- Loan repayments: if you do not know the amount, call your loan officer.
- Owner wages: often called an owner's draw, but it's the same as wages.
- Payroll expenses: don't wait until tax time when a huge payment is due. If you are unaware of the amount, call your accountant for an estimate.
- Telephone and/or internet use: you may list these separately.
- Postage and mailing: this is a cost frequently overlooked until you receive the first big bill. You should estimate an amount and set it aside each month.
- Legal costs: after the initial legal costs, you may need to consult with your lawyer periodically and these costs need to be allocated.
- Accounting costs: if this is a yearly charge, set an amount aside each month.
- Advertisement: ongoing advertisement dollars to keep your name out there.
- Cleaning and trash removal: you may do this yourself. If so, then eliminate.
- Dues and subscriptions: to keep up with business and trade news
- Insurance: even though you may pay this quarterly, set aside the monthly costs so that you have it when the time comes.

Some owners add a miscellaneous column, but I do not recommended it because this means that you have expenses that you are unaware of. Instead, set aside some petty cash that you replenish to cover the small unexpected costs. When you add all these items up, this figure is your fixed monthly expenses.

Throughout the years, I have learned to rely on special mentors in times of need or when I get into unfamiliar waters. When I started my first venture, I was totally unaware that there were those experts who could help me with my questions, problems, and other business-related issues. Since the beginning of my business career, I have built a strong and effective mentoring team at no monetary cost. Today, this team consists of an attorney, accountant, banker, an insurance agent and several highly successful businesswomen. You may include others on your team, but these are the essential mentors.

You should already have your first mentor, your attorney. The next vital mentor is your accountant. Some entrepreneurs feel that when they first start out, they can handle the financial piece of their operations. As long as you set your books using a structured system, then for a while this may suffice. If you start your business and mix your personal and business finances, it won't be long before you get into trouble, which is usually at tax time. If your financial segment is in order from day one, then you can concentrate on growing your business.

Many entrepreneurs start out with just a bookkeeper and then hire a Certified Public Accountant (CPA) firm to do their end-of-the-year tax reports. When operations are small, this is advisable. But when you commence to grow, a CPA firm has the knowledge and expertise to ensure that you're proceeding along the correct financial path.

I recall that when I opened my first business, I counted on a family member to set up my books and maintain my financial records. It wasn't long before my business began to grow, and I sought out a bookkeeper. My first bookkeeper was great at what she did, but she was quick to inform me that I needed a Certified Public Accountant (CPA) to take over because of the rapid growth of my company. She said that bookkeepers are there only to do the books, where a CPA is the trained professional who is fully aware of the ever-changing rules in the financial game.

My first CPA firm consisted of only a one-person firm because I thought that was all I could afford. Before I contracted my second year, I compared fees with other CPA firms, large and small. I learned that when a CPA firm has multiple partners, along with a large number of gophers who do the menial work of collecting and organizing financial data, that their work is done quicker and at no extra cost. In addition, the larger CPA firms have many partners with a variety of experience and expertise that can be utilized at any time, now or in the future. I've been with a major CPA firm for over seven years and have added my financial division at their recommendation. Our CPA firm works in direct concert with this division. I couldn't be happier with the results it's produced. I've shared this learning experience with those I mentor in the hopes of giving them some tips about the financial arena.

Victoria tends to go first class in whatever she does, hence selecting the best CPA firm that she can find to set up her financial division, anticipating growth early on. She shops around, asks other business owners about their experience with firms, and then sets up an informational session with several CPA firms before selecting one for her company. Victoria seems to always select a firm that is well established and one that insists on interviewing the new client to determine if they (CPA) will even take her on as a new customer.

Next, you will need to secure a bank or other financial institution to handle your business account. If you are good at what you do and your products or services are in demand, then you will quickly need to seek startup or expansion funds. Bearing this in mind, I recommend that you seek a banker before you even start your business venture. One day before you open, dress up and visit several banks that you think you might like to use. Ask if you could meet with the loan officer or manager. Let her know that since you are soon to open a new business, you are looking for a bank to do business with. Don't ask for a loan at this time, but just let the banker know who you are and what business you plan on opening. When you come back the next time to inquire about a loan, she will already be aware of your business and feel that she knows you.

Losera usually leaves her banking and loan needs to the last minute, seeking these needs out only after an acute financial problem has developed. Losera commonly brings a sense of urgency when she initially seeks out financial assistance and doesn't have the time to do any screening. Losera waits until she has few, if any, cash flow dollars and expects a bank to bail her out.

When my students are preparing their BAP and getting ready to embark on their business, the subject of insurance is thoroughly discussed as to how much is enough. Knowing what kind of insurance to carry and how much to carry is important. You must consider the following three areas: 1) the size of the potential loss, 2) the probability of loss, and 3) the resources available to meet the loss if it should occur. No business can possibly eliminate or transfer all of the risks. You must assume some of them. How you decide whether a particular risk should be transferred to an insurance company or assumed can best be handled by considering the maximum potential loss that could result. If the loss could destroy your company or cause serious financial damage, then don't assume the risk. Usually losses that occur frequently are predictable and typically small. If they can be assumed by the business without too much hardship, then they can be budgeted as part of the normal cost of doing business. Some examples are bad-debt losses or shoplifting. In both cases it is better to install precautionary measures instead of costly insurance. You should research possible insurance coverage in the following areas: fire and general property, plate glass coverage, burglary, fidelity bonding, fraud, public liability, workers' compensation, product liability, life insurance for owner, business interruption, errors, and omissions that cover injuries suffered by customers.

After identifying your insurable risks and the type of insurance that is available to cover these, decide how much of a loss that you can afford to bear yourself and what you need to transfer to an insurance company. Next, secure three bids and carefully evaluate the coverage costs by each before deciding on your insurance carrier. Also inquire if there are package insurance policies at discounted rates. My recommendation is to find an insurance company with a good reputation that can assist in your risk management planning.

It is recommended that you take the necessary action to protect your business and its assets against burglary and theft before you even open the doors. Expensive equipment and cash attract burglars. This is an area where owners must consider adding burglar alarms as standard equipment. On-site or silent alarms will deter armed robbery and burglary. Some owners have a combination of two or three different alarm systems installed. These systems warn of different types of illegal entry, as well as inform the police department or the alarm company's station. The favorite alarms are the infrared alarm and magnetic or vibration detector.

Many times an owner will also subcontract the services of a security patrol that adds extra assurance to their burglar-alarm systems. Sometimes businesses that are located in the same building opt to share the cost of a burglar security, thereby sharing costs. You can also contact your local police department to seek their advice in making your site secure. Insurance needs have to be addressed before you open your business to be certain that you are protected from fire, theft, and any other liability that could negatively impact your business.

One entrepreneur who I was mentoring a few years ago was having her grand opening. In speaking with her, I asked if her insurance policy coverage was in place and she said no, but that it would be within two weeks. I advised her to postpone the opening of her new pizzeria until her insurance coverage was approved and she got the policy in writing. She agreed not to open because, as a potential Victoria, she respected my advice. Three days after she opened her pizzeria, there was a massive fire, which destroyed the interior of her building. Luckily, fire was covered under her insurance policy. She reopened her renovated place within two months. As a Victoria, she listened, followed advice, and went on to open two additional pizzerias, always careful to have her insurance coverage in place.

Mentors are vital in helping you with every aspect of starting your business. There are many mentors who do not charge for their services because they want to give back to the community or to other women who may be struggling. Victoria often has several mentors because she either looks for specific expertise in each or she doesn't want to burden one mentor with an abundance of questions.

Since many mentors are themselves Victorias, the newcomer can learn from their mistakes. No person is an island in business. We all need friendship, guidance, and advice sometimes along the way. One thing to remember is that if a mentor offers you advice, you'd be wise to follow it or let them know why you don't.

A major mistake many women make is that they start the business beyond their means. She opens the new business, but lacks one important asset and that is operating cash. When she forgets to put aside sufficient working capital (cash), then current bills can't be paid, she goes into a cash crisis and the business begins to wither.

Without a "floating" supply of cash, a business will experience occasional convulsions that distort, confuse, embarrass and alarm everyone concerned with this business. The owner, employees and suppliers first sense the nervousness of this situation and she must take immediate action to remedy this illness called the cash crisis.

No matter whether you are applying for a loan or not, the following worksheets need to be completed so that your business can operate smoothly:
- Working Capital: The minimum amount needed to operate your business for a six month period.
- Break Even Analysis: The level of sales at which your total sales cover exactly your total costs and operating expenses; the point of zero profits.
- Projected Income Statement: A detailed estimate of income by month.
- Significant Assumptions: The rationale that you used to make these specific financial projections.
- Three Year Cash Flow Projection: Your "guesstimate" of the money coming in, money going out and your business' estimated financial status for three years.

These worksheets should be completed with your CPA and/or bookkeeper because the accuracy of these figures and estimates reflect the potential success or failure of your business.

Once you have determined how much money you need, you are ready to locate funds. If there is one single piece of advice I could give you in raising money, it is that you determine how much capital you really need, what you will do with every dollar, how long you will need this money, and how you propose to pay it back. No matter what approach you use to secure financing, you're going to need a full BAP. Once you've selected a course of action, follow it without variation and discard it for another course only when the first choice has clearly proven unachievable. If you have a business selling something that your customers can't live without, then funding can usually be found.

Practically every business experiences rough financial periods during startup and growth. Growing pains that are commonly felt soon after your opening usually start your search for additional funds.

Your financing strategies should be driven by your business goals and objectives that are outlined in your BAP and ultimately by the available financial alternatives to keep your business operating. Currently, there are more numerous alternatives for financing a business than ever before. Many economists estimate that loans remain abundant today for well-structured startup companies, with the promise of more when there is gainful growth; however, I believe that this remains to be seen in the troubled financial world of today.

In considering which financial alternatives are best for your venture, you need to draw on the experience of your CPA, bookkeeper, banker, and attorney who have already been through numerous startup ventures. It is essential that you take a professional approach to selecting and presenting your business to outside investors and/or lenders. It's wise to plan for growth before you even kick off your business and pre-sell this to your investors or bankers. Foresight demonstrates that you are an astute businesswoman. It is estimated that your chances of securing a loan under marginal conditions will improve approximately 50% by anticipating your needs early on. Once your business is up and running, careful financial management is a continuing necessity. Research reveals that poor cash flow is one of the leading causes of business failure. While planning your operations, be alert to excessive use in the following areas: inventory, fixed assets, accounts payable, and administrative costs.

Once you have your BAP developed and have a rough idea of what money you think you'll need to startup your business, it's time to dress up, go out there, and get it! Raising startup capital and financing your ongoing operation is clearly a wide-range issue. It sometimes seems impossible to separate the countless details you need to be aware of in order to put your business on a firm financial basis.

When you consider borrowing, determine what kind of money you need. A business uses four basic types of money in its operations, and your purpose in borrowing will determine the type you seek.

The first type of money is trade credit, an alternative to borrowing money to buy your inventory. It's possible to obtain a large amount of credit from your suppliers with very agreeable terms. However, it's important that you don't mismanage or misuse this valuable asset to your company. I recommend that you never let your accounts lapse beyond the prearranged terms. It will have a negative effect on both your association with your suppliers and your credit rating. I know a Victoria who has no need to borrow because she uses her trade money to purchase her inventory and routinely pays in about forty-five days. This allows her ample time to sell her inventory before she has to pay her suppliers.

The second type of money is short-term credit. Banks and other lenders will provide this type of money to carry you in your purchase of inventory for special reasons such as buying inventory early for the next selling season. Such loans are self-liquidating because they generate sales dollars. You repay short-term loans in less than a year.

There was a Losera who came to see me because she was constantly using short-term borrowing to buy her upcoming inventories. She never got caught up, going from one loan period to the next. When we discussed this, it was discovered that while she did sell the entire inventory that she bought, after paying all her bills, there were no profits realized. The solution was to cost out her product, consider all of the related costs, and then mark products up enough to make a profit. This would allow her money left over to pay for the next inventory order.

The third type of money is long-term credit. These loans are used for expansion or upgrading a business and are repaid out of accumulated profits. The evidence of this type of loan is usually in the form of a mortgage or promissory note with terms.

Recently, two partners came in to discuss their inability to take a draw from their business. They were both living on their spouses' salaries. They had paid off all their equipment by using their profits. I recommended that they take their BAP to a bank, use their equipment as collateral, and obtain funds for operating capital.

The fourth type of money is equity funds. This results from selling an interest in your business and relinquishing part of the profits to the investor.

A Victoria came in to tell me about how she was expanding her business to include a new product line. She was funding this new initiative through equity funding. Earlier, she discussed this with her attorney and CPA. She still retains 80% ownership of her business and consequently had the money to expand.

Many times owners fail to recognize the difference in these four types of money. I recommend that you keep in mind that money borrowed for a temporary purpose should be used in the profit-producing areas of your business and will be repaid out of that operation. Equity finds are those that remain in the business and increase the net worth for the owner.

Money to finance your startup business can be secured through your personal savings, family, or friends. You can seek funding from angel investors, venture capitalists, bankers, or credit union managers. You could also obtain a segment of funding from all of these different resources.

The business of raising money is largely measured by your success in convincing the financial person to loan you this money. A fairly well defined system comes into play depending upon the course you take. The best source of financing is using your own money. It is the easiest and quickest form of capital to acquire, there is no interest to pay back, and you don't have to give up control of your company.

One of the worst moves you could make in business is spending all of your liquid assets, having no dollars left to finance a healthy cash flow. I see this constantly with the Losera who opens her doors without a penny to handle her day-to-day operation. I stress here that you should never drain all of your liquid assets, but keep sufficient funds to maintain a healthy cash flow and allow for potential growth.

Angel investors and venture capitalists are quite similar in their roles. They are looking to invest in new startup businesses that appear to have a great deal of growth potential. They lend you the money, protecting themselves by taking ownership in a percentage of your business. They usually want their money back rather quickly with a high level of profit. Sometimes, the venture capitalists may end up taking the company over at some point. This is the reason for you to seek the guidance and advice from your attorney before you seek these types of investors. Angel investors and venture capitalists are different from financial institutions because banks and credit unions don't want your business; they just want the interest on what they loaned to you.

When you seek to secure a bank loan, there are three critical questions that you should ask: Does the bank have limitations on the number of loans it will approve or the types of businesses to which it will grant the loan? Do I have to maintain a balance before the bank will consider my loan? Will the bank give me a line of credit, and if so, what are the requirements?

If you seek all of your capital from one major investor, you will end up with a much smaller piece of your company. If you try to raise money from friends and family, you can normally arrange a much better deal for yourself. However, sometimes friends and family end up being difficult to deal with because they assume the role of trying to run your business.

When you go to the lending institutions, the managers may want the Small Business Administration (SBA) to guarantee your loan in order to reduce the bank's risk. The three core principles of financing your business venture are the following: more cash is desired than less cash, cash sooner than cash later, and less risky cash is desired than more risky cash. These principles seem simple enough, but many times Losera ignores them.

One major key to a successful business startup and expansion is your ability to secure appropriate financing. Raising capital is one of the most essential of all your business activities. As many of us quickly discovered, raising capital is not easy and can be frustrating and complex. If you developed a BAP, compiled financial data, and have planned effectively, then you have a better chance of securing the capital that you need.

There are several sources to consider when seeking loan money. It's essential that you research the pros and cons of all your options before making your final decision.

The first course to consider is utilizing your personal savings. However, never deplete all of your savings to avoid running into difficulty when you need ready cash for an unexpected expense or to enhance your cash flow. Establishing your credit is one way of being able to borrow money later on.

The second source to consider is friends and family. The con about this source is that family and friends commonly want a say in the business, thus hindering your ability to use your own management skills.

The third source to consider is banks and credit unions. Approval of your loan requires a well-developed BAP that you present with gusto and commitment.

The fourth source to consider is a venture capital firm or angel lenders. In turn for the loan, you give them partial ownership in your company.

One of the major concerns for business owners today is access to credit or capital. The SBA has various loan guarantee programs to provide financing for viable businesses that have potential, but can't qualify for traditional loans.

The SBA guarantees, provided through private lenders and nonprofit lending institutions, give business owners access to the same kinds of reasonably priced, long term financing available to large businesses by virtue of their size and economic clout. Financing programs provided by SBA vary according to the borrower's need. SBA loans are made by private lenders and are guaranteed up to 85%.

Initially, the private lender determines whether a borrower's application is acceptable. If it is, the lender forwards the application and its credit analysis to the SBA. After the SBA review and approval, the lender makes the loan. The borrower then must pay the lender payments according to their loan agreement.

Currently, LowDoc is one of SBA's most popular loan programs up to $150,000. Once you have met your lender's requirements for credit, LowDoc offers a simple one page SBA application form and rapid turn around on approvals of about three days. Other existing SBA loans are SBA Express, the Export Working Capital Program, International Trade Loans and the Export Express Loans. You can find out more about the various SBA loan programs by going on their web site at www. sba.gov.

Point 4 of the BAP: Owner Profile
Many times when I review BAPs, the educational background is covered while leadership and management skills are completely overlooked. These are the specific data that the loan officer wants to see in order to determine whether or not you can take the lead to bringing your business to high levels of success and growth. In addition, your expertise in the field that you plan on entering must be fully and clearly explained so that the reader has confidence in your ability to handle the field that you wish to enter.

Your BAP may include an executive summary which includes your managerial, leadership, and educational experience. Segments of your owner profile should also be included in your executive summary that is placed in the front of your BAP if you plan on using it.

Your profile should include the following data:
- Full name, address, telephone number, and email address.
- Educational background, unless you have very little, in which case you should bury it in the middle or at the end of your resume.
- Expertise in the business you are starting.
- Leadership and management skills.
- Relationship skills.
- Work history.
- Personal facts if desired.
- References are optional.

You can add anything that will assist the readers in determining that you have the skills and expertise to start up this specific kind of business. This is a summary of what you and your business are all about. It is typically no more than two pages and presented in a basic format. The typical executive summary includes vital data in a narrative brief. There are pros and cons of including an executive summary, and it is entirely up to you whether or not to start your BAP with this summary. The pros of formulating an executive summary are that the reader catches a brief summary of what this business is all about. The con is that if you have omitted some pertinent data that the reader is looking for and can't find, then you have lost your battle.

Here is an example of an award-winning executive summary written by a woman who was opening a creative photography company that featured one-of-a-kind photographic creations:

"Creative Photography by Tricia" is an artistic company that features unique creations in the realm of photography. It is owned by Tricia Frances, CAS, Creative Photographer, and will be established as a sole proprietorship in the fall of 2005. Initially, this company will be located on busy Main Street in downtown Rock City. This business is being created in response to the following market conditions:

- *Startup opportunities exist in the Mohawk Valley region to meet the creative photography needs of a vast target population.*
- *There is a need for highly creative photographers who can intertwine reality and fantasy for customers who are not being served in this overlooked market area.*
- *Current research reveals that there are numerous customers who will be willing to purchase the company's services because of the lack of quality professional photographers here in this region.*

- *Clients will continue to return for additional services because of the uniqueness and high quality of our products and services.*
- *Many potential clients have already been polled and say that they will use the company's services as soon as we open.*

The initial strategies for creating this business have been developed, with the reasonable and acceptable costs to our clients for our products and services clearly identified.

Tricia has personally spent a great deal of time and effort in researching strategies to ensure that this venture has been developed using creative, yet profit-generating ideas.

Tricia's BAP is a result of intensive study in the field of creative products specifically, meeting the company's clients' wants and needs. The supplementary design of future products has been developed so that the company may add to the current line of unique products and services. To this end, a total of $22,000 was raised from family and personal assets, which will be used to finance all of the initial equipment, supplies and advertisement costs to launch this business.

The basic components of the BAP for "Creative Photography by Tricia" are the following:
- *Competitive pricing*
- *Expansion into new market places*
- *Increased marketing and advertisement strategies*
- *Lower unit costs, thereby achieving higher profits*

The owner has the knowledge, experience, creativity, expertise, and credentials to lead, manage, monitor, and assess the ongoing operations that will lead it to success.

Recently, I was asked to review an executive summary, and I soon discovered that this woman had yet to develop her full BAP. The woman revealed that she had very little experience in the field that she wanted to enter. She was going to purchase an existing restaurant on the main street in downtown Rio, utilizing her husband's retirement funds. When I asked about the reputation of this business, she was uncertain about the ratings by the current customers. Another simple question was what was she getting for her money. When the research was completed, it was found that the restaurant had poor ratings on food and services. In addition, what she was getting for $75,000 was equipment with no warranties, tables and chairs that she was going to discard, and an obsolete sign in a leased building. We quickly agreed that her executive summary needed work, but most importantly, she needed to step back and analyze what she was doing. This could be accomplished by developing her BAP.

After analyzing the situation and developing her BAP, she decided to take two major steps: to hire an experienced cook and to open a new restaurant a few blocks away with new equipment, new furnishings, and a highly creative image, all for the same price. Many times I see women jumping into situations before they have done their BAP, a move that ultimately leads to failure. It is poor judgment to begin with an executive summary when the BAP is where you need to start.

When I first decided to take my home-based business out of the house and into an incubator site, I knew that I needed money to equip the office and the training center. After calculating that I needed a loan of $15,000, I knew that the banker would want to know about my own personal worth and whether or not I could handle this loan. Thus the assets and liabilities came into view. In calculating what I was personally worth, I listed everything that I owned, including the car which was half paid (asset = $10,000), the current value of my house minus what I owed (asset = $25,000), the value of my life insurance policy if I cashed it in (asset = $17,000), my jewelry (asset = $1,500), and some antiques that were appraised at $1,000. All of the figures totaled $54,500. I was amazed at what I had accumulated over the years. The other side of the coin was what I owed. All I really owed was about $4,200 on appliances that were purchased the previous year. My net worth was calculated at $50,300. I was feeling very good when I went to the bank seeking a loan of $15,000, which was granted at the first request.

I would like to stress here not to hide any bad credit situations because the loan officer is going to find out anyway. The banking system is a network of close working individuals that can find out anything about anybody. If you happened to hit a financial snag then tell the loan officer what you did about resolving this. I find that many women have had their credit ruined by a messy divorce, whereby the spouse had incurred debts and left the wife with a bad credit history.

Through the years I've heard that the loan officer who reviews your loan request makes a decision that is 80% subjective and 20% objective. This means that the strength of your BAP along with the dynamics of your presentation to this loan officer has the power to cause your loan request to be granted or denied. I can personally say that many of the loans approved for our students are based upon the subjectivity of the loan officers. Many times, loan officers have told me that they approved a loan because of gut feeling that the borrower would never fail. Perhaps, it's the strong BAP, the structured planning that is revealed to the loan officers when they meet with the borrower. Or yes, it may just be gut feelings. When preparing your BAP, remember to include all of your past financial history in a chronological order so that the loan officer has a trail that can be followed to determine your current net worth.

I remember one woman who wanted to open a beauty salon because she couldn't find a job. She had the experience and expertise to operate this type of business but her credit was very poor due to a recent divorce. She was able to show the loan officer that she was paying her bills on time, and that if she opened her salon, she would make more money than if she worked for someone else. When she went for her interview with the loan officer, she dressed for success and appeared to be successful. Her first impression led to securing a loan to set up her salon, and ultimately, she created a successful business venture. We can never underestimate the first impression that strikes at the core of the loan officer's decision-making process.

Early one morning I received a surprise visit from a Victoria, an outstanding graduate of our recent entrepreneur training program. Victoria was planning on opening a computer repair shop soon. Suddenly, she burst into tears, saying that she was afraid, (of what, she didn't really know) but she definitely was not going to open her business. I asked some simple questions to calm her down because I frequently see this fear of the unknown exhibited by women. We established that the startup costs were going to be minimal because she had all of the necessary tools. Then we discussed what she would lose if the business should fail. I seldom like to talk about failure, but sometimes it's needed, as in this case. She said that there were no anticipated losses that she could think of except the cost of a one-year lease, which she could handle.

Victoria and I discussed her vast computer expertise and the fact that money wasn't the issue here. She also had her back up team of two computer savvy brothers ready to help. We decided that she should find a location and continue her planning activities. Eight months later, Victoria launched a multidimensional business that included a computer training school, computer hardware/software outlet, and her repair shop, all in a busy urban area. The fear of the unknown is one of the major obstacles that I see in women. I have found through experience that reasoning it out is what it takes to get them back on track.

Another Victoria who had difficulty dealing with the unknown was a recent divorcee. She was going to use her divorce settlement to purchase a bed and breakfast (B&B) because she couldn't stay in her current home due to the sad memories. She purchased a five-bedroom home in a beautiful rural area that was ideal for a B&B. Her greatest fear was that she would lose everything. My first question to her was, "How much would it take to renovate this home?" She replied, "Approximately $15,000." She had more than enough assets to handle the purchase of the B&B and these renovations. She developed her team of mentors, completed her BAP, and opened her B&B in nine months. One year later, she is happy operating an outstanding B&B.

Point 5 of the BAP: Competition
I recommend that you address the following nine questions:
1. Who are my competitors? It's imperative that you are aware of competitors and their impact on your business at all times.
2. Where are they located? Remember to check the Internet for similar competitors. The Yellow Pages are also a great place to start researching your competition.
3. What are their strengths? Many times we think that we are indeed the best when it is a false security. We can learn the strengths of our competitors and try to replicate these.
4. What are their weaknesses? We can learn from weakness so that we can avoid them.
5. What can I learn from watching my competitors? Knowing is better than guessing and that is what you get when you watch your competitors at all times.
6. How many competitors do I have? Many times Losera tells me that she has no competitors. But once she starts searching, she is amazed at what she discovers.
7. Are your areas saturated and in no need for a new business like yours? This takes a great deal of research, but in the end you will know whether or not your business is needed.
8. How much does each competitor charge for similar goods? We want to push our profit margin to what the market will bear. This is one strategy of finding out what customers are currently paying.
9. Which competitor is most challenging? I like to think that all entrepreneurs will observe their leading competitor, and then take the best strategies of the competition and apply them to their own business.

I've noted that Victoria thoroughly studies her competitors that appear prosperous in the hopes of discovering their secrets to success. She regularly designs her operation to serve the customers even better, offering them still more than her competitors. Victoria researches similar businesses that have closed their doors, particularly those that have gone bankrupt. She wants to learn what made them fail so that she can avoid similar pitfalls.

Competition is healthy, but you have to know who your competitors are up-front in order to determine their negative and positive impact on your operation. If your competitors are currently servicing the same customers that you are targeting and they are treating them well, perhaps, you won't have enough customers to make your projected profits. Now if your competitors are poorly servicing their customers, then you can start offering better products or service and attract their existing customers along with some new ones of your own.

Losera continuously says that she doesn't have any competitors. I've come to sense that it's her inability to conduct appropriate research to identify them. Losera just overlooks her competition and tries to handle it later on when it rears its ugly head. Victoria views her competition as a red flag in making money. Victoria is aware that she is competing for the same customer base and she wants her fair share, perhaps more.

The above responses to competition should be converted into a narrative about each competitor, which will be included in your BAP. You should include profile summaries for at least four of your major competitors.

May I recommend that you frequently meet with your mentors to discuss your competitors. They can help identify and explore the strengths and weaknesses of your competition. The rationale is that too many effective competitors may negatively impact your venture. One point that I would like to stress here is that all competitors impact your bottom line. You must constantly keep an eye on their activities in order to be superior.

Along with exploring how to start a business and creating your BAP, there is an innovative exercise that can greatly benefit your chances of success. You need to set aside some time to make an on-site visit to a business similar to what you are opening. If your business is unique, then select another type of business in your locale to visit. You will visit this business, assess their operations, and learn from what you have observed. You will research and draw conclusions about the following:

Exterior Observation:
Signage: visibility, size and colors.
Windows: attractive or not, cleanliness and/or limitation.
Parking: ample spaces, safe, near entrance, easy access, handicapped spaces.

Interior Observations:
Initial Greeting: warm, cold, happy or lacking greeting completely.

Lighting: bright and cheerful or dismal.

Displays: messy, neat, products and/or services displayed.

Pricing: high, low or just right.

Choice of Payment: accepts all types of payment, some types or only cash.

Employees: friendly, rude, indifferent, difficult to locate.

Owner's Physical Presence: Happy, rude, indifferent.

Advertisement: where did you learn about this business?

Promptness in customer service: Excellent, good, poor or uncertain.

Overall Impression:

What part of this business would you replicate?

What areas would you improve?

This simple exercise can be performed over and over again and will allow you to change and modify your operations. I would recommend that you do an on-site visit to one of your leading competitors so that you can learn new ideas and techniques to make your business operation even stronger.

CHAPTER THREE
Managing Your Business

Setting Up A Plan For The Management Of Your Business:
Once you have dealt with the first five points of the BAP (Business Action Plan), you need to move on to the sixth point. The sixth point is setting up a plan for the management of your business. I recommend that it's time to examine your leadership and management skills. Now you will have to begin to make important and prompt business decisions in order to successfully lead and manage your company. Victorias tend to rapidly cultivate and use effective leadership and management skills because they realize the impact these have on their success or failure. Through the years, I've discovered that Loseras seldom think about leadership and management because they're too busy telling everyone how difficult it is to run a business. They seem to anticipate that failure may be on the horizon.

Leadership skills are vital when you have to take initiatives to lead your company to success. Numerous researchers say that the best approach to leading a business is through total employee involvement. I strongly urge you, as the owner of your business, to keep the final say in making major decisions. When it comes to changing the way your business is run or when you need to spend a great deal of money on a new piece of equipment, you as the owner should make the final decision. Of course, you can take input from others, weigh its value and consider the options in your decision-making efforts.

As novice entrepreneurs, Victorias usually examine their leadership skills, polish them up and gain new skills that will allow their business to thrive. Victorias carry on with their strong belief that they are going to succeed and they will let nothing get in the way of their business success. Over the years, I have viewed Loseras as the exact opposite. I constantly recommend to Loseras to stop whining about the skills that they don't have and concentrate on the skills that they really need to succeed. Then plan on getting these skills from reading, workshops, mentors or hiring an expert in this field. An essential part of formulating your venture is to work on BAP point six. Point six is formulating a management plan for the new business venture.

Point 6 of the BAP: Formulating Your Plan

At no time in your life will you need strong management skills as when you go into your own business. If managing is foreign to you, then I highly recommend that you acquire a manager who can mentor you and bring your business along. It is possible to learn a lot about managing a business by taking a seminar, workshop or skills management course. Every business is different and will require different management styles. You have to try out the various styles and then decide which style of management brings the most effective results to your company's operation and the bottom line of bringing in profits.

One of the essential management skills that will impact your success is learning how to manage your time. You need to define goals, objectives and the tasks needed to achieving your goals. Often I hear women say that we don't have enough time, but there are exactly 24 hours in each day and we all have the same amount. It isn't a matter of not having enough time; it's how we manage it.

Managing time means controlling our most critical resource because that's what life is made of. It is critical to know what we want do, set priorities and use time to our best advantage if we are to succeed in business. There is no secret or magical formula in changing your behavior to succeed in time management. All you need is real action instead of wishful thinking. You must see the pay offs derived from effectively managing your time.

I feel that everyone knows how to manage time, but then why don't we? It's because really managing our time effectively means doing something. Instead, most of us procrastinate because we don't know how to start, don't know where to start, don't like what it is we have to do - and the list of excuses goes on and on. The more intelligent we are, the more we can find ways to procrastinate and prolong the agony of not achieving our goals. My first recommendation is to start by setting goals and their related objectives. Next, prioritize these and it's not so difficult. Prioritizing starts with identifying first, what you must get done now; what you need to get done soon; and what would be nice to do if you have some time left over. Then start somewhere or anywhere in taking action to achieve your number one priority. I find that many Loseras work backward, doing what they like first and avoiding the important things.

Victorias always seem to know that time is money, but Loseras seldom value their time, but live in a world of chaos. Loseras aren't planners of time and unconsciously squander it every chance they get. Victorias use their time for generating money and try everything that they can to save and wisely allocate their time in order to achieve outcomes. Loseras seldom identify their outcomes; consequently, they are lost from the start.

Through the years I have recorded five tests of the initiatives displayed by successful women. These are inner drive to get the important things done, ability to fully accept doing the most important things (even if they don't like these), a tough-minded attitude, a drive and focus toward excellence and a well thought-out plan of action to be accomplished. These women plan to be efficient and prioritize in order to be effective in the use of their time.

I have seen Victorias create their daily "To Do List" and go on to eliminate their time wasters. They have methods to effectively consolidate activities that seem to go together, like making three phone calls at the same time. Victorias take pride in delegating anything that someone else can do for them. This frees them up to do important things, like generating new or unique ideas.

I have noted that most Victorias tend to recognize positive and negative work hours. This is the simple theory that positive hours are productive ones and negative hours are unproductive. Some people are morning people and some people are evening people. These categories are based on the times when a person is at her peak in making decisions and are at their top in her productivity cycle. Women should discover their most productive times. This is done by thinking of the time of day that you really like to work and the times when you feel least productive. Victorias appear to have the ability to recognize the differences between productive times and unproductive times and apply this awareness to their time management plan. They utilize productive hours to handle the most important aspects of their business, particularly the decisions impacting the overall business operation and specifically their profit margin.

I know one Victoria who identifies twenty-five time wasters at the start of each year and eliminates them as fast as possible. She thinks in terms of managing time and making money in everything she does. Victorias can turn the bitterness of failure into the sweetness of success by constantly utilizing their time management skills.

One of the greatest time wasters is a disorganized office. Someone once said that a disorganized office reflects a disorganized business. Steady flow of papers such as mail, bills, reports, faxes, and journals present a challenge to keeping your office organized. Is it any wonder that you have trouble finding your desk when so many papers arrive daily? Unless you keep on top of organizing your desk, the clutter of papers can become overwhelming. So if getting a handle on the paper beast has been on your mind, perhaps now is the time to tame it with my five steps. The most difficult step is the first one and that is getting started. The first step to getting the paper beast under control is to clear your appointment book for at least four full hours and start the clean up process. To make certain that you don't get calls or interruptions, you may want to do this when your business is closed. The next step is to take all the files and paper stacks from the floor, your desk, on top of cabinets and anywhere else you've creatively managed to store the paper jungle and make one big pile. Have a large trash box ready for the battle that is about to take place. Sit down and prepare to go through each paper one by one. You have one of five things that you can do with each piece of paper:

1. Throw it out
2. Do it
3. Read it
4. Pass it on (if you have someone to pass it on to)
5. File it

Incoming mail can be a problem if you are the only one in the business. The cardinal rule is to handle incoming mail only once, if at all possible. This helps to break the negative habit of wasting time over handling your mail. You can reply immediately, delegate to someone else or discard it if no reply is necessary.

Label four boxes to sort your mail into and then leave the fifth box for trash only. The difficult part is to just sort through all your paper. Don't read, don't stop to call or write a letter, don't file, just sort. Just keep what is necessary for running your business. Since it is hard to know what is necessary you must use the probability of use theory:

Problem: Should I file or discard it?
Probability: What is the probability of my needing this information again? Risk Taking: Make a guess estimate if you are not certain you will need this information.

Considerations: Is it available somewhere else (try not to look now, just guess)? Is it estimated that you will throw away about 30% of all incoming mail? When all the papers are sorted into the four boxes, it is time to take a second look.

Start with the "Do It" box. Does it really have to be done? Is it unimportant? If so, then throw it out. Further, do I really want to do this or can I pass it on to someone else? It may be that it is too late to respond to a particular piece of mail. If it is too late then dump it. It is important to ask yourself, can I handle this with a telephone call? Can I write my response right on the paper and mail it out or do I quickly draft a letter? I suggest that you have a red pen handy so that you can put a red dot on each piece of paper that you handle. Soon you will have to do something with this piece of paper you keep picking up because now it has the measles and it bothers you. If you discover a thick report decide whether it is worth reading or not. Skim through the table of contents of each journal and mark the articles that you feel are important. Reading these will become your nighttime, lunch hour or leisure activity. Now prioritize your reading material, starting with the most important piece. When you did your first sorting, you were sure that some of these papers should be filed. Now take time to reevaluate because approximately 80% of what you file will never be looked at again. With this in mind decide whether to file it or trash it.

Now you can go back and tackle your four small boxes. You may not be the trash collector's best friend, but you will no longer feel lost in a paper jungle. You have not tamed the wild paper beast. Constantly fighting the paper beast does not have to be a way of life. Don't let it get the best of you again. Set aside time on your calendar regularly to tame the wild paper beast, especially when you can't find your desk because it's lost in the paper jungle.

Recently, I received a call from an office secretary of an interior design company seeking my help in getting her boss organized. If the boss didn't get organized, then she was quitting. The initial visit to the office revealed a complete disaster area. When one desk got so buried with paper, a new desk was brought in for the boss. We agreed to start the task the following Saturday. While going through papers, I found a check for $1,000 that was six months old and another one for $500. Jokingly, I told the boss that my fee would be only the checks that I uncovered. At the last count we had located over three thousand dollars in buried checks. Once we cleaned up the mess, I asked why she let this get so out of control. She replied that she hated being cooped up in an office and wanted to be out in the field like the early days. It was decided that she would hire an office manager, allowing her to get back to her first love - interior design. She went from a Losera to a successful Victoria within a year.

Running an orderly business necessitates keeping an orderly desk. Keeping clear unambiguous financial records connected with the business is essential. Your books must be set up so that your personal money and that of your business are completely separate. I highly recommend that you initially hire a Certified Public Accountant firm. I couldn't do without my CPA firm, which has knowledge of the current rules and regulations and possesses the expertise to keep my records current and correct. Keeping business records is important not only because it is required by law, but because it is essential for running a business.

You must keep records of your invoices and bills because you need to prove that your expenditures are legitimate. You must procure a checkbook. It must include a description column for recording to whom the check is issued, the date, and what the check is written for. The invoices or bills can be stapled behind the check stub and when the bank clears the check, it can be stapled to the invoice. This can be placed in a file that is designated for bills paid.

One area is maintaining an accurate and well-planned cash budgeting system, which is vital to the financial security and viability of your company. This will let you know how much cash you have on hand so that you can compare it to current expenses. If, for any reason, your cash on hand is not enough to pay your expenses it will result in a negative cash flow. You may be able to sustain losses for a short period of time, but if you continue to run a negative cash flow for very long, you will eventually have to close the doors.

Cash flow is a critical element that is frequently overlooked until it is too late for business survival. In order to have an adequate cash flow you start with a yearly operating forecast. Let me clarify that the cash flow and operating forecast are not the same. You can make money, but it is not always in the form of readily available cash that is required to operate your business. Primarily, the value of the forecast is to allow you to preview anticipated profits and expenses for the upcoming year. The forecast is also a control tool because when your forecast is completed for the year, you can compare actual figures along the way. When your estimated figures appear out of line, you can make changes early on.

To get the most of out of your forecast, you should make important estimates and they should be as realistic as possible. You begin with what is coming in (revenues), what is going out (expenses), and how much money you started with. There are two important steps that I recommend: begin by identifying all of your expenses such as fixed expenses that include rent, utilities, telephone, insurance and salaries and then add any other expenses that have surfaced. Then project a reasonable estimate of sales by determining the amount you expect to sell in products or services each month and what dollar amount you expect to receive. After these estimates are made and entries are totaled, you can then compare the projected results with your desired profit goals.

You should keep track of your income, expenses, what you owe people and what others owe you. Payroll records, tax reports and payments all have to be recorded and tracked. Tracking your inventory is a must in order always to have enough on hand for your customers, yet not more than you can sell.

If you see that expenses are not going to be covered or too little profit will be realized, then changes can be promptly made. Consider making changes if goods and services are priced too low, there's too much inventory, sales are too low, and interest or payroll is too high.

Once your business is underway it's time to monitor your company's progress. There will be a constant state of change and hundreds of variables that will come into play everyday. Each of these variables will pull you one way or another, right or wrong, depending on how you deal with each one. How is it possible to implement the most effective strategies to handle the hundreds of variables that emerge in your day-to-day operations?

I strongly urge you to develop a clearly defined Annual Strategic Plan that includes how you will measure your key performance outcomes. How you manage and monitor your operations will result in whether or not you meet these performance objectives, which leads to your successful operation. The majority of these outcomes are closely related to your financial performance that includes sales, profit margins, and your accounts receivables. Other variables that may impact your operations are the number of customer complaints, positions of your inventory, sales figures and status of your accounts payable.

The development of your Strategic Plan and the related performance measurements will support your management communications and monitoring throughout your company and they become the keys to your long-term growth.

To measure your success through performance outcomes, compile a list of the specific factors that have the greatest impact on your profit margin sales such as current cash flow, sales growth, measurement of profits, customer feed back and employee feedback (once you have it). Then you can begin to monitor your weekly cash position, cash disbursements, accounts receivable, and accounts payable, new sales and any backlog of orders. Other variables that impact your operation are the cost of administration and the number of employees in relationship to sales. These two variables should be monitored and measured on a monthly basis.

Since there are so many variables in business you should have a floating supply of cash. A business will experience convulsions that distort, confuse, embarrass and alarm everyone concerned with the business. The owner, employees and suppliers first sense the nervousness of this situation and the owner must take immediate action to remedy this illness called the cash crisis.

Another important strategy for business efficiency is the frequent delegation of responsibility. Delegation is seen as a must for all Victorias. As mentioned earlier, Victorias never do anything someone else can do for them, but they also monitor all of the progress as well. On the other hand, Loseras usually demonstrate ineffective delegation, whether because of mistrust, fear or just lack of ability to do so.

Another way of maximizing your time is to make use of interns. I've learned of many Victorias who approach local colleges to see if they have a program where an intern is assigned to companies free of charge. The general purpose of this internship is a learning experience at no cost. Many times I have seen Victorias taking advantage of these intern programs. They feel that they have acquired another valuable team player at no cost to their budget. Loseras seldom think out of the box like Victorias do when trying to find new and unique money saving ways.

We know that operating your own business gives the owner the freedom to do or not to do the things needed to become successful. In the first year, Victorias usually work between forty-five and sixty hours a week and know where their time is spent. Loseras can be found taking long lunches; closing early to play golf and doing other mundane activities that harm their business. I recommend to Loseras that they acquire management skills to develop their strategic management plan.

It is my thought that implementing effective meetings can make or break your business. Working meetings are one of the best ways to handle problems, issues, concerns, motivation, the securing of information for policy setting, and the communication and disseminating of information.

Years ago, I created the "Who's Got The Z" method for handling meetings. Prior to every meeting, one of the staff is assigned the "Z" on a rotating basis. This person is responsible for developing the agenda of events, running the meeting, appointing the timekeeper and ensuring that there is a recorder. The "Z" is the leader and controls all of the meeting events. The "Z" controls interruptions by closing the door, preventing telephone calls, having water/coffee in the room and handling other interruptions. The "Z" also facilitates managing arguments, limiting the monopolizers and keeping uninvited people out. As mentioned earlier, all staff members assume the "Z" role and this leads to their taking pride and ownership in running these meetings.

A rule that I profess is that if there is no agenda, there is no need for a meeting. If the meeting was important enough to arrange, then the activities should be clearly stated and recorded. Distribution of minutes should be timely and feedback encouraged.

The majority of Victorias control their business operation by conducting regularly scheduled meetings. Even if they are the only person on their team, they can and do hold weekly meetings. They set up two extra chairs and imagine that people are sitting there who they can talk to about their operations. This is how Victorias get ideas flowing and it helps them to start identifying and handling problems. I know one Victoria who invites her brother and sister to weekly meetings to discuss growth initiatives and then rewards them by buying dinner.

The meetings by Victorias are structured and held at least once a week. There is always a note taker. New business matters are discussed and anticipated outcomes are projected that will be discussed at the next meeting. Notes are retained in a specific notebook and Victoria appoints someone to be in charge of its safety.

I feel that one of the major reasons for meetings is to address the business operations as a whole and to generate new ideas about how to make the company more efficient and effective. Planning meetings are an important element of Victorias' success. They identify their business goals early on and then outline the related objectives and actions to be taken to achieve these goals. Victorias seem to have an inner drive to getting things done by sorting out the important elements, maintaining a tough-minded attitude, striving for excellence and prioritizing their time and those who work for them.

The next area of real concern in operating your own business is the high stress level that goes with it. Of all the processes of human life, stress is probably the most researched subject in the world, yet the least understood. There are thousands of definitions of stress found in today's research. The most frequently quoted definition is that stress is the result of a person's response to pressure. The Merriam-Webster's Dictionary states that, "Stress is a strain or a straining force, mental or physical tension".

Never will you have so much stress as when you go into your own business. This is a direct result of the excessive number of changes involved with operating that business. Change is thought to be one of the leading causes of stress.

After completing my doctoral dissertation on stress and ten years of stress research, I made a simple definition of stress as pressures on the outside causing you problems on the inside. All people are different so that life events affect them in different ways. Stress is part of the very fabric of life and is as essential as eating or breathing.

Those like Victoria appear to handle the everyday stress in their lives very well. Going into your own business has been compared to taking a roller coaster ride with a blindfold on. The thrills are many, but the stress that is produced is even higher. Moliere once said, "The greater the obstacles, the more glory in overcoming them". This holds true in business and in everything that you want to accomplish.

There is only one time in your life when you are free of stress and that is when you die. You must have some degree of stress to stay alive. Stress can be good or bad, depending on how you interpret it. You could equate stress with the playing of the violin: when the strings are in tune it plays well, when they are too loose the violin sounds terrible and when they are too tight they will snap. This is the simple analogy of life and stress and is applicable to real situations. You need just enough tension to become productive, but you must be aware of the point when it becomes a negative impact on you or your business operations.

One of the major stressor you will encounter is people. Victorias tend to evaluate stressful people as to the impact that they have on their business and go on to take control over the stress that is created. Victorias feel that the more control they have over their everyday life events, the less stress they will experience.

I feel that a problem is like a monkey on your back that causes you stress. The more problems that you have, the more monkeys you carry on your back. You have to feed them, clean up after them, besides carrying their weight. No one likes to admit that they have a problem. The first step in coping is to change the problem into a positive objective and to identify the action to go with it. I feel that unfailing belief is the strongest ally that Victorias have in achieving success.

A noted Victoria told me that once she had a major problem of not making enough money to successfully operate her business. She shared with me what she did about this dilemma. Victoria turned this negative problem into a positive objective by stating (and firmly believing), "I'm going to make money". Immediately, she started applying the rules of making money by finding new customers, better serving the current customers, advertising more and costing out her products to be certain that they were profitable. In doing this, she took control of this financial situation early on and found new and innovative ways to generate additional money. Throughout her career, she continues to call upon her strong belief that she can make as much money as she wants and needs.

There is no doubt that stress comes into your life every single day, hour and minute, but as long as it leaves, this stress will do you little harm. It is the lingering stress that creates your internal problems. Therefore, in order to take control of your life, you must take control over the bad stress that occurs.

I recommend the following eight strategies for coping with stress to all women, but usually the Victorias are the ones who heed my advice and reap the rewards:

1. Handle one "monkey" at a time, get rid of it and move on to the next one.
2. Worry less, because the things you worry the most about usually never happen.
3. Bury yesterday's mistakes and learn from them.
4. Develop a network of business friends to turn to in times of stress.
5. Refuse to think "old" because you can do anything you put your mind to.
6. Remember that time is money and if you waste time you will lose money.
7. If you can't face or flee, then float for awhile and reexamine your problem.
8. Surround yourself with positive people and "fly" with the winners.

The Victorias have coping traits seldom found in others; they look for outcomes in everything they do and the rest seems to fall into place for them.

One characteristic frequently demonstrated by most Victorias is that they regularly plan some fun and don't feel guilty about it. Victorias seem to know that a well-rounded balance of work and play makes for a less stressful life. Sometimes, Loseras too have a fun event, but then they are so overloaded with guilt that they seldom repeat it.

Busy holidays bring in stress along with the changing seasons. The holidays are far more stressful for business owners because of a number of reasons. There are late inventory deliveries, a winter storm predicted, employees calling in ill on the big sale weekend and the list goes on and on. There are the irate customers who are tired of shopping and take it out on you. Victorias just listen, nod their heads and try their best to serve them. They play soft music and put out tea and sweets to help ease their customers' holiday stress.

What really happens is that the stress of holiday business alerts you to its danger. This causes your adrenalin to increase - a fact that results in a burst of energy and Victoria makes the most of it. The pleasure of seeing throngs of customers excites Victorias and produces a healthy type of stress that they take as positive. On the other hand, Loseras view the increase of customers as a very stressful time. They let it create a business environment of stress and chaos, leaving negative feelings for everyone along the way.

One of the best remedies for handling stress by Victorias is to admit that the holidays are the time of year when things do get out of control and stress does strike. Victorias find relief from their stress when they count the profits from increased sales and know that it's all worth it.

There are ten holiday coping strategies that Victoria applies:
1. Make the number one priority serving your customers and making additional profits.
2. Relax and smile because a smile is like a fine perfume that becomes a fragrance throughout your store.
3. Admit to yourself, your family and friends that you are only human and can't be everything to everybody during this hectic time.
4. When a crisis occurs during the holiday rush, Victoria asks herself if this is a matter of life or death, if not, then she rolls with the punches.
5. Expect messes at this time of the year and when things slow down next month, Victoria will clean them up.
6. Enjoy the holiday changes as opportunities and not as threats. Victoria sees the rush and changes as something very exciting and positive.
7. Involve family in the long work days by having them help out at the store, wrapping presents for customers, greeting customers as they walk in and then enjoying a relaxed dinner at the end of a long day.
8. Let family and friends, share in the good and the bad of the operations during this hectic holiday rush.
9. Forget your diet and try to get as much sleep as possible. Wake up thinking happy thoughts, wear colorful attire, plan something special after the holiday rush and focus on what you do best - taking care of your customers.
10. Take time to notice the most joyous time of the year and anticipate perhaps, a miracle or two.

The ongoing stress that all entrepreneurs face throughout the year is compounded by the fact that without involving your family and friends, the stress is going to be much more severe because of the lack of this support system. I strongly recommend that when you begin to plan the start up of your business, you build your immediate support system to turn to in time of need.

Women often face stress over balancing family duties and business even more than men do. Although increasingly men share the responsibilities of rearing children and other domestic duties, women usually are called upon to bear the brunt of these responsibilities. Balancing your home, family and work isn't easy, but it can be a challenge to your ability to prioritize not only your business, but your personal life as a whole. As part of my ongoing mentoring duties I have a program called "Excelling As A First Time Woman Owner: Trials and Tribulations of Balancing Your Life." Many times, I say to women that if you organize your day the rest is all child's play. It is important that your husband be just as supportive of your career as you are of his. My children were very supportive, as long as I kept them in the loop of knowing what was going on in my busy schedule. My son has earned a reputation as an outstanding chef. My daughter assumed the role of organizing my business and personal calendar. She has become a manager of time far more efficiently than I have ever been. She prides herself in helping employees in my office, enabling them to accomplish more than ever expected. As a woman business owner I still prioritize almost every day of my life in order to get the most out of my time. I ask my family for help and it's amazing what they will do for me. I recommend these strategies for you in order to blend your business and personal responsibilities and get the most out of your life. Since there is never enough time, you need to employ the quickest way to accomplish these tasks. It is important to consider how many children you wish to have. Allowing intervals between their births will certainly make it easier to balance domestic responsibilities with work. Since you are the manger it should be possible to arrange your schedule on a flexible basis so that if a crisis arises at home you can be free to attend to it. Before going into my own business, I was a full-time Nursing Instructor, a doctoral student, and the single parent of two teenagers all at the same time. This appeared to present a monumental challenge, but I learned to prioritize everyday, every hour and almost every minute! Because of the pressures on my time I had to stop watching television for several years. Watching television was not a high priority for me. I received excitement in my life, however, when I got an "A" grade at the university. Personal achievement is more rewarding than being a couch potato. Having a good manager to supervise the business when you are called away will help relieve your worry about the business. It is helpful to locate your home as close to your business as is feasible. Then you can be in touch with both business and family. Some women take a leave of absence from their occupation upon the birth of a child. The first two years seem especially demanding of the woman's attention. As children enter pre-school and kindergarten, part of the pressure is lifted from the mother's shoulders. Sometimes, though, the husband will take a leave from his job to nurture infants. Of course, many women lead a single life and others choose not to have children. Still, others enter business after the child-rearing experience.

One of the dangers of excessive and prolonged stress is burnout. Burnout can be caused by the following factors: long hours, overwhelming business obstacles and just the stress of competing over the years. Burnout is a destructive syndrome that slowly creeps up on people who care too much about their commitments. With burnout comes negative attitude, a feeling of continuous exhaustion, life loses its meaning, and job helplessness and high irritability doesn't go away. No matter how exciting owning your own business can be and how dedicated you are to the success of that business, there is the danger that arises from the truth that too much of a good thing can be too much. Therefore, you need to guard against burnout. To guard against burnout you might want to follow the following words of advice:

- Set realistic goals, become a sharp scholar and think out of the box.
- Be confident on the outside and handle challenges on the inside.
- Be positive in all that you do - that's half the battle.
- Take charge of your business and your life.
- Balance your work and play so that you have a well-rounded life.
- Learn from your mistakes, bury them as "learning experiences".
- Don't let the business consume you...get a life!
- Be passionate and have a sense of pride in what you do.
- When stress strikes, you can fight, flee or float, so use this selection.
- Celebrate success, no matter how small.

Remember that stress is your body's reaction to a demand made upon it and if left unresolved, then burnout will creep in.

I recall one woman who came to me the week before her Grand Opening because she felt overwhelming panic. I was very surprised because before this time she had set up the business, completed her BAP and performed all of the necessary activities to successfully launch her business. We sat and talked about her fears and soon we uncovered that her fear of failure was the number one problem. We proceeded to explore all of the possibilities of failure and discovered that she lacked a support team to turn to in time of need. Presently, she was "going it alone". We called her daughter in Philadelphia, her mother in Wisconsin; both immediately came to her rescue, giving her the initial support she so desperately needed to embark on her business venture.

Let's move on to another area and that is networking. I have found that one of the most overlooked ways to promote yourself and your business is by networking. I'm not talking about NBC or CBS, but about the ways of meeting new contacts to promote you and your business venture.

Networking with strangers can be scary, but on the other hand strangers are no more than friends you have yet to meet. How many times have you let your imagination get the best of you like the times everyone was talking to each other and you stood there alone or the time that you were afraid that you had said something wrong and made a fool of yourself. We tend to avoid networking opportunities because we're lazy, we don't know how or it makes us feel uncomfortable. Actually, it may be the fear of the unknown.

Many times part of the problem is letting your imagination get the best of you.

Walking into a room full of strangers can make you anxious and can give you a stomach full of butterflies. Perhaps, you can take comfort in the fact that many people share the same networking fears.

If you have effective networking strategies and are prepared, you will be successful in the network arena. You can walk away with valuable contacts through networking if you have the right kind of attitude and preparation.

Here are ten networking hints to follow:
1. Seek opportunities to meet others who can help you in your business. A Business Forum, workshop or club meeting can open new doors to meeting professional people.
2. When in a group, practice speaking slower because most of us talk too fast. Lower your voice an octave because most women tend to talk high pitched fashion when we get nervous and our audience senses the fact.
3. Get yourself ready. Forget your anxieties by concentrating on other people; they probably have the same anxieties as you.
4. Prepare some small talk and have at least two questions in your mind to open the conversation such as how long have you been a member of this group or what do you do for a living. These open-ended questions will lead to further conversation.
5. Always dress the part of success, because you operate a highly successful business. Put your best foot forward because you never know whom you are going to meet.
6. Have some impressive business cards ready to hand out. The strategy to getting your business cards "out there" is to ask other people for their cards and automatically they will ask for yours.
7. Look for opportunities to network. If you see a group coming into the meeting, join them and enter into the conversation with a big smile.
8. If you have to wear a name tag, take your own personal one along. Make it one that is impressive such as gold finish and easy to read.
9. Look for people who you think are approachable. Make eye contact with them and if they look away, then perhaps those are the avoidable people and just move on. Look for someone who appears uncomfortable and usually striking up a conversation will be easy.
10. If you are going to find a place to sit down, find a table where only a few are sitting. You will find them happy to welcome you. They probably haven't gotten into deep conversation yet so you can join in too.

Now the time may come when you lack networking events, but there is another strategy to handle these times. Everyday, make at least five telephone calls to potential or current customers. Perhaps you can invite a potential customer to lunch and this will pump new blood into your customer base. Ongoing networking can be beneficial to both new and established businesses owners alike. With daily persistence you can make new contacts and they can be of great value to both you and your business. The more you do it, the easier it gets and the rewards of networking will follow. Future success belongs to those who dare to network.

As you progress in your business venture, there will come a time when you need help and this usually means hiring employees. I would like to go on record that you are not to hire an employee until you have a well developed, clearly written job description. I say this because without a job description, I find owners running around trying to get things done, while employees are running around trying to find something to do. Think about this: would you go on a trip through a foreign country without a map? Then how can you expect employees to do their jobs without their map called a job description?

Here are four basic criteria to consider in the selection of an employee:
1. *Informational Factors:*
   Review vocational interests, mental abilities, knowledge, skills and judgment. Does this person have most of these traits?
2. *Motivational Factors:*
   Economic security, recognition and achievement, position, prestige and power. What is this person's personal code of ethics and relationship to others? Does this person have the necessary drive to provide her with incentives to do the job well?
3. *Behavioral Factors:*
   History of work habits, stability, perseverance and responsibility. Has this person developed the basic work habits and good character traits that will make a desirable employee? How will she fit in with our existing team?
4. *Attitudinal Factors:*
   Personal attitude, social attitude, other attitudes and frustrations. Does this person's attitude indicate that he can make satisfying adjustment and accept change in the workplace?

Once you start hiring employees, it is time to develop an Employee Handbook. There are many resources that you can find and use at very little or no cost, so don't reinvent the wheel. Many times you can turn to an Entrepreneur Center such as ours and it will share a generic Employee Handbook model that you can easily adapt to your company.

One area that you should be alert to is spotting grievances because unless they are

addressed, it may lead to worker dissatisfaction and employee turnover.
Here are my 25 Causes of Grievance to watch for:

1. Unguarded and ignored work hazards
2. Favoritism
3. Ignoring complaints
4. Unexplained pay shortages
5. Complicated wage payment system
6. Tampering with piece or job rates
7. Giving orders without giving reasons
8. Loss of earnings due to bad tools or equipment out of order
9. Poor planning that interrupts and cuts earnings
10. Unequal distribution of overtime
11. Withholding credit
12. Treating employees unfairly
13. Lack of personal interest in employees' welfare
14. Reprimanding employees in front of others
15. Broken promises
16. Unhealthy working conditions
17. Unequal pay for equal services
18. Inadequate instructions or training resulting in mistakes and blame
19. Stealing credit for employees' ideas
20. Ignoring suggestions
21. Too many rules and regulations
22. Placing employees on jobs for which they are not suited
23. Uncongenial team players
24. Penalizing employees for conditions beyond their control
25. Failure to promote from within

When you do decide to hire employees, educate yourself or seek assistance. You will need to inform yourself on how to best hire, meet rules and regulations covering employment in your location and how to maintain the necessary employee records. My final advice to you as an employer is to treat all employees the same. If not, then you will hear the word discrimination, which gets more employers into trouble then any other reason.

Early on, I said that some women go on to be very successful entrepreneurs, while others fall by the wayside. One of the major traits that I have noted in the successful Victorias is motivation. I define motivation as an action process that encompasses the person as a whole. The causal categories are ability, luck, effort, mood, illness or fatigue, early experiences, control and intentions which influence motivation, along with interpersonal stability.

There are three methods of motivation:
  1. Fear motivation is negative reinforcement:
  This form of motivation is through punishment and is unacceptable.
  2. Incentive motivation is giving a reward for desirable behavior:
  This method is unpredictable because it stops when the rewards cease. Employees come to expect the rewards and have difficulty being motivated unless they are rewarded.
  3. Attitude motivation is the most workable system:
  This is based upon the satisfaction of individual needs and has proven to be long lasting.

Just as I have talked about your need for motivation, so must your employees in order to achieve your company's goals. When you begin to hire employees you must create an environment that breeds motivation. Here are my five strategies:
  1. Get acquainted with each direct subordinate.
  2. Give them someone to look up to (you).
  3. A subordinate wants and needs recognition.
  4. A subordinate needs someone to help her over the obstacles.
  5. A subordinate needs to feel confident that she is top-notch.

All companies desire and hope for highly motivated people and good management depends on achieving your company's goals and objectives, with the help of a motivated team. I find that Victorias create such an environment.

The following are my six keys to motivation:
  1. Ask for performance:
  Clearly describe the job, give the written job description and discuss the performance outcomes expected.
  2. Use lots of positive reinforcement- and personalize it:
  Don't take acceptable work for granted. Thank people for it and praise them every time that they improve. Remember that what motivates one person may leave another cold. Find out what works with each person.
  3. Build relationships:
  This doesn't mean being buddy-buddy with your employees; it means that you should treat people like real live human beings. That is what they are and they will respond best when your actions show that you respect their individuality and trust their intentions.
  4. Understand your employees' point of view:
  Make a habit of listening to your employees and ask their opinion before you give directions or offer advice. If you listen with an open mind, people are more likely to cooperate when you decide things have to be done differently.

5. *Model what you want:*
   Approach your work with a sense of urgency, use your time efficiently and meet the goals that you set. Demonstrate to your employees that the job really does matter and show them by your action.

6. *Refuse to accept poor performance:*
   Although few researchers studying motivation readily admit it, managers do have to tell employees when their performance is unacceptable. Sometimes, this means a reprimand. At other times, you can handle it with retraining or coaching. I recommend to everyone that it's better to aim for excellent and hit good than to aim for good and hit average.

Many times, we have to admit that employees who comprise our team may fall short of expectations. Through the years, I have noted that it may not be because they lack motivation, but because their leader is moving faster than they. In our fast pace, we forgot to let them know about the new outcomes that we expect. I used to assume that those around me knew what outcomes we were supposed to achieve and these assumptions have gotten me into trouble. After several wake up calls, I have changed my way of thinking by including those around me in our everyday activities either by informative meetings or one-on-one sessions.

There is one important area that I emphasize for all small business owners to become aware of and that is the Occupational Safety and Health Administration's Hazard (OSHA) Communication Standards. According to current OSHA statistics, over forty million workers in all types of jobs are potentially exposed to one or more chemical hazards. Chemical hazards pose serious problems because they can cause kidney and lung damage, heart problems, sterility, cancer, burns and allergic reactions. Many chemicals can cause fires and/or explosions and other serious accidents. When your employees are exposed to these chemicals, grave illness or injuries could result.

The major goal of OSHA is to ensure that employees are aware of chemical hazards and how to protect themselves. This knowledge will help to reduce the incidence of chemical-source illnesses, disease and injuries that are rapidly increasing every year. OSHA establishes uniform requirements to ensure that the hazards of all the chemicals used throughout the country are evaluated. The hazard information, along with protective measures must be sent to employers who then share it with employees.

Labels on containers and material safety data sheets (MSDS) must accompany all hazardous materials. In addition, employees must have hazard communication programs that make employees aware of this information. The employees should also establish employee protection programs if needed.

As a business owner, you must be aware of the OSHA rules and regulations and determine if these apply to your company. You must continuously be aware of all the chemicals being used at your site. When you go into business, call OSHA for their guidelines.

I recommend the following seven steps to comply with OSHA:
1. Read and make certain that you understand OSHA standards and know your responsibilities as an owner.
2. Walk around your site and check to ensure that all potentially hazardous materials are properly labeled.
3. Establish an OSHA file that includes a list of hazardous materials used in your business, where they are being used, a copy of the MSDS sheets and make everyone aware of where this file is located for easy access.
4. Develop procedures for updating the OSHA file.
5. Make certain that you have all of the MSDS for all chemical substances used.
6. Take steps to ensure that all containers are properly labeled, tagged and marked.
7. Develop and implement a written OSHA Communication Program at your business for employee training and as a protective measure.

Your company may not have hazardous materials, but by acquiring the knowledge about OSHA standards you will be able to react immediately to chemical hazards.

This brings to mind the time three women came in to discuss opening a company that would manufacture hand-made soaps and beauty products. They had no idea where to begin to address their fears about customer use and the associated liability on their part. Currently, they have customers eager to buy their products, but have many liability-related fears. I recommended that they immediately seek the advice of an attorney about the extent of their liability with these products. In addition, they need to research the ingredients and their level of safety. Approval for the use of their specific products should be discussed in depth with their attorney who can direct them to the next step. I highly recommend that when you are dealing with products that can cause any type of customer reaction that you thoroughly assess your level of liability. Then, immediately discuss this with your attorney and determine whether or not it's worth the risk to launch this type of business.

Next we will discuss three important areas of managing business - how to manage a family-owned business, buying an existing business and selling your business. Even though these three areas may not apply to your business now, perhaps, you can learn something from reading this chapter to use in the future.

One of the most common questions of concern that I have when talking with someone who is opening her own business is, "Are family members going to be involved in this operation?" If the response is yes, then the work begins! The owner must start off on the right foot by being prepared in specific areas. Like any other business operation, employees must have the qualifications to do their job, well defined job descriptions of what each employee does is a must and periodic evaluations that are objective and conducive to positive change must be made. These are only a few of the challenges that need to be addressed to avoid family problems emerging.

Management problems occur in every business, but when it comes to our business instead of my business, then the problems are far different. When family members come together to operate a business, emotions frequently interfere with the decision-making process.

Conflict and problems sometimes overflow into all facets of the operations when relatives observe the business from different viewpoints. If relatives are stockholders or silent partners, they tend to put profit-making activities far above capital improvements, purchase of needed equipment or investing in needed inventory. Sometimes relatives will frown upon hiring, even though it is vital to growth. Some are reluctant to put any of the profits back into the business. Problems are further compounded if the relative has no talent for money or business.

When relatives are directly involved in the daily business operations, they tend to consider major issues in light of growth, production sales and employees. For the person who has to manage the family owned business, the most important factor is to recognize the confines of relatives' emotions and make every attempt to keep them under control. Many times it's difficult to assess a relative's skills and abilities when another relative is calling them lazy and undependable. Emotions not only affect the family working together, but other employees too. Uncontrolled family conflict tends to spread like wild fire to all those in the business.

If you are selected to manage the family owned business, then you had better be assertive and tough enough to handle bickering and personal conflicts, because they are inevitable. In addition, sound management practices are a must for your business success and here are a few tips to help you.

1. *Manage by the Business Action Plan and a Vision:*
   Have you identified realistic goals, objectives and related tasks? Is everyone working toward profits and growth?
2. *Develop an Organizational Chart:*
   In the family business, you may need just a simple chart that shows the

chain of command and accountability. This may be enough to harness questions about who's in charge.

3. *Start with Jobs descriptions:*

Family members will have a clear understanding of their jobs if job descriptions are in place. Job descriptions may not help prevent conflict with your relatives, but such details can help in resolving misunderstandings.

4. *Never do anything that someone else can do for you:*

If you are designated as the manager, then refrain from routine tasks that can be done as well, if not better, by other employees. You are there to manage the business and make the decisions that will influence the success or failure of that business.

5. *Take action to reduce costs:*

Family members should come together regularly to brainstorm about reducing costs. Costs must be kept in line to continue a profitable operation. Quality, service, excellence and attention to customers should always come first. Is overtime necessary and under control? Can changes be made to better serve your customers and make more profits?

6. *Outline policies and procedures:*

The best products and services in the world can run into difficulty in distribution policies and procedures are not right for them. One strategy is to check on your competitors to see if they are operating more efficiently and effectively.

7. *Plan for succession in the event of your inability to operate the business because of ill health:*

As the designated manager of the family owned business, it is up to you to make certain that a smooth transition occurs if something happens to you. The successor may not be the same person that fills in when you are away or ill. The family should address this issue ahead of time in order to groom the successor.

Every manager has to work hard at initiating and maintaining sound management principles, but this is even more difficult when family members are involved in the business operations. As the managing relative, you should be well trained and have a support system in place. In the end, operating a successful family owned business is a challenge, but this is one way to guarantee that your family members have jobs. It will also enable your family to leave a legacy that others can look up to. Always remember that when the going gets tough, the tough get going and this is truly important when operating a family owned business venture.

Recently, two sisters came in to discuss their fears of opening their own business. Both of them were unemployed due to a company downsizing. They wanted to open a Senior Service Company, rendering home-care to senior citizens. Their greatest fear that held them back from launching this business was what if one of them became ill or wanted to leave the business.

They lacked a formal BAP, so I recommended that they start there. In addition, I advised them to contact an attorney and have a Partnership Agreement drawn up. This would clearly detail how the business and/or their partnership could be dissolved. Armed with the BAP and a Partnership Agreement, both sisters are actively operating a highly successful business.

In addition to the option of creating a family owned business, you may run into the possibility of purchasing an existing business. Buyers usually have one of three motives:
1. Market diversification - access to new technologies or new markets
2. Financial gain
3. To buy the business and operate it (the most common)

Buying an existing business can be a simple shortcut to establishing your own business, but it has its pros and cons that need to be discussed with your attorney, banker and accountant.

To determine the selling price of a business, a valuation assessment report must be prepared by the seller and reviewed by the buyer. This report eliminates the guesswork and the painful trial and error method of pricing.

Businesses are frequently purchased lock and stock, including equipment, fixtures, inventory and office supplies. As the buyer, you can easily go off course by selecting a business that is already ill fated, perhaps in a less than desirable location and/or has a poor reputation.

Recently, a woman came in to discuss purchasing an existing business and had questions about the hazards of this type of venture. There are many reasons to buy an existing business and just as many for starting your own from scratch. What I recommended to this woman was to find a successful existing business that you want to imitate and ask for a Business Valuation Report. After reviewing this report, put yourself in the owner's shoes and you now have a viable blueprint for success. The real issue of buying an existing business involves a lot of pros and cons that starts with in-depth research.

One woman wanted to buy an existing Sports Bar for what she assumed was a good price. Then she came to our office for advice on how to obtain her liquor license. Renovations were well underway and new furniture was ordered. My first question was: "Do you have a variance from the Codes Department to open as a Sport Bar?" She was baffled and said that the realtor made no mention of this. She assumed that because it was an existing Sport Bar that she could also open the same kind of establishment. Other questions that I asked were, "What was the reputation of this Sport Bar and how did the adjacent homeowners feel about it?".

She soon discovered that the existing bar had a reputation of being noisy and rowdy. The neighboring homeowners had been unhappy about these activities for a long time. If she requested a variance from the city, it was quite certain that the neighbors would vote no and she would be unable to open.

She stopped renovations, went to the Codes Department and had to go through a public hearing at which time she didn't receive approval to open her Sports Bar. She came to me and we put our heads together and turned lemons into lemonade. She redirected the renovations and converted this three story building into four top-notch housing units. These units were all rented and she has recently purchased the house next door that will soon be converted into additional rental property.

There are distinct advantages in buying an existing business.

If the following are documented, these become the rationale for a purchase:
- Acquiring an existing & established business operation
- Acquiring a customer base
- First-class employees
- Premium inventory
- High quality equipment (with warranties), at a good price
- A first-rate reputation and track record

On the other hand, there are disadvantages to buying a business.
Some disadvantages of buying an existing business are:
- History of poor employee relations
- Old and obsolete inventory
- A business that is over-priced
- Caters to the wrong type of customers or the owner takes them
- Undesirable location
- Previous owner has a bad reputation or poor credit

It is essential that you make certain that your banker, accountant, and attorney are all involved from the very start.

There are five basic strategies for evaluating the possible purchase of an existing business.

1. Assessing the three-years financials, inspecting the federal tax records and looking over the state sales tax records:

One important question to ask is the following: are you qualified to assess the accuracy of the existing financial records of this business? Most of us are not, so it's best to hire someone like a Certified Public Accountant who has the expertise. They will critically evaluate the assets of the business and decide how much of the information is sound and correct.

The seller will quote sale figures. These must be verified by checking the sales tax records and purchase order copies for the past six months. Of course it's a lot of work, but it needs to be done. This will help you check the cost, age and estimated value of the current inventory.

2. Good will of the seller:

Talk with the seller's customers, bankers, neighboring business operators and suppliers. Ask each of them about the seller's reputation for quality, service, integrity and honesty. If the seller isn't willing to give you the names of these contacts, then quickly walk away from this deal.

3. Ask the question; "Why do you want to sell"?

Consider this response seriously. Does it appear to fit in with all the other information that you gathered? Does it seem genuine? Does it make sense to you? If these answers leave you some doubt, probe further. Ask more questions and don't be shy because it's your hard earned money that is on the line.

4. What are you really getting for your money?

Has the local Codes Department been contacted and is there a variance in place so that once the purchase is final, you can operate the same kind of business? Just because the current business is operating as a café doesn't mean that you can purchase it and assume that you can operate a café too. Your attorney is truly needed here to ensure that the Codes Department agrees that your variance is in place.

The signage comes with the deal, but are you going to change the name and add another unexpected cost? Are the furnishings what you really want or could you do better by purchasing new ones?

Other areas that many women overlook when buying an existing business are the safety issue, ample lighting and parking, handicapped accessible (a "must" to open) and whether or not the majority of existing customers will remain with you or flee.

5. What's left after the purchase?

Consider what you are getting for your money and would you be farther ahead starting this business from scratch? One area that you should be concerned about is whether or not there are warranties covering the major appliances. Also, you must look at what your cash flow will be once the final payment is made and whether or not you have ample cash to operate the business.

When it comes to the closing, a buyer's source of financing depends in part on the size of the business to be purchased. Many times a smaller company can be financed by the buyer who has the down payment and adequate working capital. The borrowing complexity of each project is different. If the purchase can't be financed by the buyer, then outside financing may be sought from an institutional lender. After looking for all sources of funding, the buyer may apply for a bank loan to complete the acquisition. It's almost certain that personal collateral will be required to acquire the loan for your purchase.

In addition, you need to assess whether or not you will have enough money left to see you through the wild economic realities you will surely face. Calculate your *Return On Investment* (ROI). This is the projected net profit revenues minus expenses over the price of the business plus the added investment needed = ROI.

One thing to remember is that most suppliers will want to get paid at the time of delivery (COD) until you have established your credit. The question becomes whether or not you can afford to pay for your entire initial inventory and needs up-front. Look at competitors and determine what they are doing differently than the present owner. If you change operations, would it be more profitable?

The research in buying an existing business is time-consuming and costs money, but it is worth it in the long run. The results can save you from disaster. If all factors are equal, working your way through the research of buying a business versus starting from scratch will make you that much wiser. As long ago as a hundred years before Christ, a Roman said, "Let the buyer beware." It's no different in today's world of business than in the past.

Change seems to be the law of life. There may come a time when Victoria wishes to move to other or greater business ventures. Of course, since life is uncertain, she may become ill and unable to continue operating her business. Of course eventually Victoria will want to retire and sell the business in order to provide funds for her retirement.

For numerous women, their business is the vital piece of their retirement account so that they can retire and live in their usual life style. If they don't add value to their business over the years, then they are gambling with their future. I recommend to all women that they monitor the investment value of their business. A valuation will provide a point of reference as to whether the sale of your business will allow you to retire in the style that you desire. Many professionals such as real estate brokers, financial planners and Certified Public Accountants offer valuation services. If you have a close relationship with your accountant and attorney, then they are your best source for adding credibility to your valuation report.

A sound valuation should identify the unique qualities of your business, the tangible and intangible assets, combined with the current marketplace sales data. Your intangible assets may include customer lists, quality and trained employees, vendor lists, intellectual property, brand identity and any other data that makes your business unique. The tangible assets are anything that is part of the final sale such as equipment, the office set up, and inventory. A valuation is no guarantee of success in getting your future-selling price, but the valuation process can be your wake-up call that changes should be made now.

The years seem to fly by and before you know it the time has come to sell your existing business. It's crucial to prepare years in advance so that the sale of your business brings you the compensation that you want, need and expect. One area that I have a real concern about is financial records. You should keep only one set of financial records and they should be accurate without padding. When you are ready to sell later on your financial records should not be negatively distorted, no one wants to buy a company that is generating little profit. The true value of your company depends upon the current condition of your facilities/equipment, financial records and the profit potential of your operation. When you get ready to sell, in order to attract buyers, your business has to reflect that it is making money.

You can find potential buyers by advertising through the media or trade magazines. Attorneys and accountants sometimes are aware of buyers and perhaps, a customer or investor may want to consider buying your business. To evaluate your company you will need to furnish a current income statement, balance sheet, three-year tax returns, sales journals, customer index, financial ratios, legal issues and any other data related to selling.

The structuring of the sales transaction may include asset versus stock transactions, leverage buyout, seller-financed transaction, earn-outs and or a stock exchange.

Once again you will need the assistance of your accountant and attorney when selling your business. The accountant can help you determine the worth of your business and can assist you by documenting that your business is worth the asking price. The attorney will assist with all of the paperwork and confirm how and when you will get paid from the sale of your business.

John Dunne wrote, "No man is an island" many years ago which still holds true today. Once Victoria had her support team in place, life and her business were headed for success and continues to this day.

Now we will address calculated risks and what the impact of risk taking has on your business operation. Initially, we will discuss problem solving and the techniques that I will recommend for you to consider when making calculated guesses to solving problems.

As carefully as you may have followed your BAP, life has a way of throwing curve balls into your original plans. It therefore is wise to prepare for these unexpected crises by formulating contingency plans.

Many successful women utilize contingency planning which has benefits such as forcing you to explore the possible consequences if things do not go as planned. If you must change your plans, then you have identified alternatives with less risk.

There are Five Steps to your Contingency Planning:
   1. Ask, "What can happen to my plan?"
   2. Estimate the probability of this happening.
   3. Compute the consequences of the event to your plan.
   4. Take action to reduce the probability of the event.
   5. Prepare for the occurrence of the event and list alternatives.

Some feel that contingency planning is disaster-oriented, but really is it so bad to become aware of obstacles and problems while you are planning?

One area that is commonly found in the lives of Loseras is crisis management. Crisis management means reacting to problems as they occur, rather than anticipating them and taking the necessary steps to avoid or limit their consequences. Researchers feel that crisis management is the second world-wide time waster. Loseras usually have a work-day of dealing with crises and "fire fighting", with little time left to plan. When managing your business, I highly recommend that you seriously consider Murphy's Law that states that if anything can go wrong, it will, nothing is as simple as it seems and everything takes longer than you think.

Here are four coping strategies to combat crisis management:
1. Sound planning with flexibility built in.
2. Continuous monitoring.
3. A pro-active approach rather than a reactive one. Avoidance of over reacting.
4. The anticipation of problems to avoid them and to limit their consequences.

Victorias usually sit down before starting a new product or service line and perform a "what if" scenario. They ask themselves, what if there are too few customers, the profit margin doesn't meet my expectations or the sales of the product or service is below the norm.

They explore what crisis could occur and then list probable alternatives and/or solutions. Sometimes Victorias decide not to launch the new product or service until additional research is conducted to ensure success.

CHAPTER FOUR
Operating Your Business

Once you have set up the structure of your business, you will be faced with operating it on a day-to-day basis. All your plans will come to naught if you do not implement them in the actual running of your enterprise. Since you are in it for the long haul, you will need to be consistent in implementing all your Business Action Plan's (BAP) points.

Inventory is needed when products are being produced. If inventory is not needed, such as in the service business, then you can omit this point.

Point 7 of the BAP: Selecting & Handling Inventory
One of the most obvious aspects of doing business to most women is purchasing their inventory. Inventory can take many forms such as finished goods, raw materials and/or goods in process. Any type of inventory means that your money is tied up and can't be used elsewhere in your operations. Inventory refers to anything needed to do business.

Many times Loseras tie up all of their money and this proves to be a disaster. There are "just in case" and "just in time" inventory management styles. "Just in case" means lots of inventory on hand that may not move and "just in time" is limited inventory that can be easily replenished, if the need arises. In today's competitive world you had better learn and practice "just in time" management when it comes to buying your inventories. Victorias ask themselves important "just in time" questions:
- Do I need all of the inventory that I planned to order? If I don't get it now, then can I get it fast enough if the need arises?
- What inventory is a loser and should be eliminated?
- What can I eliminate and yet fully service my customers and still make a healthy profit?

Victorias learn to manage their inventory well in order to make a profit. Unless inventories are controlled, they are expensive, unreliable and inefficient. Profits will only be realized when inventory is sold and money goes into the cash register.

You can't afford to absorb the losses arising from poor inventory control because money is tight for most small business operators.

Many Loseras tend to keep their inventory on the high side and this leads to a lower rate of return on the dollars invested. Successful inventory management means a fine balancing of the cost of the inventory with the benefits of maintaining this level of inventory. Carrying too much inventory represents not only money tied up, but also additional costs of storage, insurance and taxes. Many times, fewer inventories can increase your cash position to the point that you have more working capital without borrowing money.

The number and kinds of inventory records you maintain depend upon the type and amount of your inventory. In small businesses, visual control is commonly used, whereby written record keeping is only needed for the slow moving or expensive inventory items. As businesses grow, they need more formal inventory records that in some cases attempts to improve inventory management and reduce final costs. This may still fail; not because of insufficient records, but because of inaccurate and careless record keeping data.

Many businesses use inventory tags, the cards system and/or accounting data to maintain their inventory tracking and control. As the numbers of items grow, the time will come for you to consider a computerized inventory control system. The first questions to ask yourself are: should I purchase an in-house system and do it myself or do I employ a service company to do this work. Today, more than ever, inventory control computer systems are within your reach. There are numerous computer companies that will do the work for you at a reasonable cost. You could purchase your own computer-based inventory system, but the main question is do you have the time and expertise to handle it?

One frequently used measurement of inventory control used by Victorias is the inventory turnover rate. This is a rough guideline by which Victorias set goals and measure performance. It is important to remember that turnover rates vary with the type of business, the kind and purpose of your inventories and how the rate is calculated. Some Victorias base their inventory turnover rate on just sales and others on goods sold.

Many Victorias use values that are calculated and published by trade associations or professional groups. Then they can use these values in setting guidelines for their particular business operation. However, Victorias frequently and carefully review and consider the accuracy of these published values.

I once heard someone say that you should keep your friends close and your enemies closer. I recommend that you apply this rule to managing both the amount and kinds of inventory that you buy and determining how much you will charge for each item.

Watch your competitors (enemies) and take the lead from them. You want to buy inventory items that will sell at a price that will make you a healthy profit. Visit your competition and try to learn what sells and what doesn't sell.

There is no better way to determine your inventory than by asking your customers what they want and what they need. Then ask your suppliers how long it takes to get a reorder and judge the amount of your order accordingly. Your judgment comes into play here and you may not always be on target, but that's the risk we businesswomen must take. My rough rule is that when inventory is over a year old, its worth about 50%. If inventory is over two years old, then put it on sale at a price that will recover your cost. I recommend that you find out how long it takes to replenish an item and determine when and how much to order. Inventory ties up money and you want to avoid this if at all possible.

The constant threat to retailers is that some items won't sell. Here are a few helpful hints to move your goods.
- Poll your customers constantly about their needs and wants.
- Know your customers by name.
- Always try to have enough employees to handle your customer load and this takes constant observation on your part.
- Never let a customer walk out without buying something until you ask what they are looking for or what can we get you.
- Be alert for items that are new and innovative and select a choice few for your inventory testing.
- Train your employees how to effectively sell and how to serve the wandering and undecided customers without pressure.
- Identify a creative team member to design and decorate your window displays.
- Watch your competition at all times and offer something better than them.
- Ask your employees to wear or use your inventory items to get ideas of what sells and then ask them for feedback.
- Get the security experts to help you avoid product theft.
- Have everyone smile and greet customers.
- Serve your customers promptly and efficiently.
- Why not ask your customers what you could do better because they seem to have the answer.

Some of the most frequently used contradictions for controlling inventory that result in disaster are:

- Keep your inventory low, but don't sacrifice servicing your customers.
- Obtain lower prices by buying in volume, but don't end up with slow moving stock.
- Maintain a wide variety of inventory, but don't spread it too thin on the rapidly moving ones.
- Use strategies to increase sales, but don't forget your customers' wants and needs.
- Have adequate inventory on hand, but don't have too many of the "lost leaders".
- Be profit-oriented, but don't forget to keep the shelves well stocked.

Some closing hints are: combine your purchases and avoid duplications, become a comparative buyer, confirm all orders in writing to ensure the price and shipping time up front and check what you receive to make certain that it's what you ordered and of good quality.

From control of your inventory to the control of your products is but a degree away. Victorias always take steps to ensure that their employees know the importance of selling the products that are the most profitable. They make certain that the most profit producing goods are available and ready for their customers at all times.

It is important to manage the inventory of your business carefully. When you start thinking about buying your inventory it's important to remember that you want to secure quality inventory at a price that is reasonable. It is also important that the inventory be up-to-date and appealing to your particular customer base. This is why you must consider what your customers will buy and at what price. Many times I've seen women buy the inventory that they like, forgetting about their customers wants and needs, only to get trapped with thousands of dollars worth of aging inventory.

This is what I recommend that you do when buying inventory: secure three prices for all types of inventory and do a comparison of quality versus price. However, I would never sacrifice quality to save a few dollars, but this is your call.

Later on, you may get so comfortable with your suppliers that you become remiss in shopping around for three prices. I think that this is as a big mistake on your part and could lead to buying at more of a cost with less of a quality.

Here is a visual format for controlling quality and price.

Each item or group of group of items must be listed with a unit cost and then the total cost as shown in the example below:

ITEM	UNIT COST	TOTAL COST
100 Vases	$3	$300
100 Pots	$2	$200
400 Shipping Cartons	$1	$400
12 Rolls of Wire	$7	$84

This list continues until your entire inventory is identified before you can begin to shop around to secure three bids.

Victorias are the women who know every aspect of controlling inventory, employees, resources, collections and customers. They are well aware that these important elements result in their business success.

One feature used by most Victorias is the continuous use of the sale sign in their windows. People will always be attracted to sales and it is best that you find some lost leader to put on sale at all times.

When goods are over one year old, then they demand to be put on sale. If you can recoup the cost of these goods, then you're lucky. If goods are over three years old, they will probably never sell. You may want to donate them to goodwill and take the tax write-off.

Victorias always know how to compete. They watch their competitors, are alert for new styles and products and constantly, poll their customers for new wants and needs. Only in doing these things can they be successful because the retail business is tough and only for the strong willed owners.

You must have a return policy in place before you even open the doors. It is best that you look at the major stores and how they handle the return of goods and follow suit. Victorias always make certain that all of their employees know and follow the same rules of returning goods. The customer is always right and if you have to make a questionable refund once in a while, it is better to refund than to lose a customer. Seriously consider your approach to unhappy customers. The damage that they can do to your business image by telling others that you are unfair can be overwhelming.

The next important area of concern for all small business owners is the quality of your products and services because this is what keeps your customers coming back. Many Victorias put into motion a Total Quality Management (TQM) plan before they even open their doors.

My definition of TQM is a program to measure quality of your products and services from the onset. It also gives confidence to your customers that the quality you provide today will be provided again and again. TQM is a philosophy of doing business that focuses on customer satisfaction, a program that increases quality of your products or services and a device that once implemented correctly can separate your company from your competitors.

I recall one woman who owned the Pizza Parlor where I frequently ordered pizzas. I began to notice that no two pizzas were alike. If Anne was working, the pizzas had twice as much cheese and very little sauce (not to my liking). When Helen was working, the pizzas were just what I wanted, with standard cheese and sauce. Customers like me desire consistency and want to know that we can get the same type of pizza no matter how many times we order it. I recommended TQM be applied and so Victoria called her team together and said that every pizza going out will be made the same way. To test the theory, she randomly selected a pizza during each shift to determine if it met the standards of TQM. Victoria soon discovered that at least three pounds of additional grated cheese was used per day when Anne made the pizzas. TQM not only resulted in a consistent pizza going out but savings in the cost of ingredients.

The rationale behind implementing TQM is that successful companies increase productivity and morale by using TQM measures. In addition, with the fierce competition out there, TQM retains customers and attracts new customers because of their consistent quality products and/or services.

I recommend that you:
1. Begin by reviewing and defining what outcomes you want to achieve to become TQM savvy:

TQM really means that when products go out to your customers, they are top quality and have had to be made only once and are perfect by the standards that you have established.

2. Implement consistent processes:
The process of rendering goods or services should be consistent at all times. Look at the methods Wendy uses to make certain that all of their fish sandwiches are served by the same top quality method. If a fish sandwich is inferior, they have methods to discover this before it is served to their customers. Suppose an

employee puts twice the amount of tartar sauce on the fish sandwich and perhaps this customer expected it the same way she got it yesterday. She is so disappointed that she will not come back and, alas, a customer is lost.

3. Remain flexible to changing needs:
Costs of materials go up and if your prices never change so that pretty soon you are operating in the red. You must monitor all the costs that are part of costing out your product or services and realize this early on. Prices must be raised in small regular increments and not just every five years.

4. Utilize documentation to track progress:
I strongly urge you to use the "management by roaming" style. This means that you continuously roam around your site to observe what is exactly going on in all areas of production. If you render services to customers in their home, then visit your employees on the job at random times to observe what they are doing or not doing.

Let your employees know how to take care of your customers from day one. Remind yourself and employees everyday what I profess that; "Customers are made of gold and if you have them then you've got a gold mine". I'm frequently asked: "What can I do to retain and keep my customers happy?" Listen, listen, listen to your customers and take it from there. Ask them; "How am I doing and what can I do better?" When you ask: "Is there a new product or service that I could provide?" It opens the door to customer communication.

"The customer is always right" is my motto and I have lived by this for over fifteen years. Yes, sometimes you may lose money on a product or service through a customer complaint, but with TQM it won't occur too often without getting immediate attention.

Victorias keep a critical eye on the age of their inventory and take action. They roughly assess that if inventory is over one year old, then it's worth about half the purchase cost. The inventory that is over two years old is estimated at a worth of about one third the purchase cost. Victorias assume that after three years they might as well donate it and take a loss. I sense that this is their basic rationale for monitoring what doesn't sell and what does and adjusting their purchasing according to these simple rules.

Recently, I met with a Victoria who had a dream of opening a Bridal Shop in a busy downtown mall. Victoria had the experience and expertise because she had worked in a bridal shop for ten years until the owner died. She had no desire to buy this shop because it had been badly neglected over the past two years and needed an entire face lift. In addition, the current location was poor.

She had savings that would cover everything, except about half of her initial inventory. While working on her BAP, she dressed up one day and visited three bank presidents, letting them know that she was going to open a first class Bridal Shop soon. Six months later, when she returned to these banks, the President remembered her and referred her to the Loan Officer. When the Loan Officer learned that the President referred her, she received special attention that led to her successfully receiving a loan.

Once you have secured the proper inventory you need to institute a proper pricing system for the goods you wish to sell. The goal in pricing a service or product is to do the following: mark up your labor and material costs sufficiently to cover overhead expenses and generate sufficient profit. Loseras repeatedly fail without realizing that they price their products and services too low. It's great to establish your prices on these two elements, but you need to consider whether the market will bear your prices, whether your costs are accurate and whether your competitors are underbidding you. A business that does not generate an adequate profit level is more vulnerable to failure because it lacks the cushion that good profits provide for absorbing costly mistakes. However, price is a secondary consideration when genuine expertise is involved and unique products are offered.

When you are figuring the costs you must be sure to consider all the overhead expenses that your company faces. Overhead can be divided into fixed and variable costs. Fixed expenses are those that must be paid, usually, at the same rate regardless of the volume of business and these costs occur every month such as rent salaries, insurance and legal costs. Then there are the variable expenses. Expenses that change according to the amount of your business such as printing, packaging, shipping, acquiring extra supplies and other variables.

In determining the price, you must compute your gross profit margin that is the difference between net sales and the cost of those sales. Thus if Gross Sales total $1,000 and the cost of sales is $300, then the net profit margin is $700. Then when the operating costs of $140 are deducted, the remainder is $560 net profit before taxes.

One of my restaurant owners, a Victoria, said that last Easter she had taken too many reservations that caused a hardship for her chefs and especially the servers. This upcoming Easter, she was going to raise the cost by seven dollars per person, hoping to reduce the number of reservations. Instead of reducing the Easter count, Victoria received two hundred and fifteen additional reservations. This supports the assumption that price isn't everything when attracting customers. We discussed the increased numbers and she realized that this could be turned into an opportunity and not a problem as she thought earlier. We determined that if two and a half hours and an extra chef extended the serving time and two more servers were added, this workload could be easily handled. More customers came and $5,375 additional gross profits were realized on this Easter Day.

Pricing your product or service has one of the most important impacts on your profit margin, more than any other element. Pricing must be high enough for you to make a profit - it's as simple as that. Yet it's so difficult for most Loseras.

When costing out your product, you add the cost of the materials used to make the product, plus the packaging and your time. Here is an example:

Cost of a floral arrangement: flowers = $5, vase = $1, ribbon & wrapping = $2 and the time it takes to make it = 1 hour x $12. The total = $20.

The charge to the customer should be double the cost or $40, but it would be best to charge $39.95 to entice the customer.

It is a little more difficult to cost out services. You have to consider the number of hours of your time or that of your employees involved and the cost of whatever supplies that you may use. Here is an example:

Cost of cleaning a house: 3 hours x $12/hour = $36 total and we used $1 worth of supplies. Double the cost = $74, but this may be more than what the market will bear. It is difficult to compete in some areas, but if your work is exemplary, customers will usually pay. Before Victorias reduce their price, they cut the hours and do less work.

Some trade associations have a schedule for service charges. Check with your trade organization for your line of business. These figures can become your yard stick to make certain that your prices are competitive. If you can't be competitive then take another look at your services and what is wrong with your pricing. Consider travel time if this is going to eat into your service time and profit margin. Remember that time is money. Also, consider charging mileage, but check out whether your competitors do and follow their lead.

If you can't charge enough to make a healthy profit, then perhaps you can't afford to make the items or render the services. The bottom line is profits. Victorias constantly review and adjust their fees by carefully reviewing everything associated with pricing to ensure an acceptable and usually an above average profit margin in everything they do.

About three years ago, a young woman named Barbara came to see me because she was going to open the College Coffee Café in order to become her own boss. She wanted to learn how much to charge for the coffee, scones and pastries that she would be selling. This led to a series of questions about her business venture. It seems that she was graduating from college in two months and couldn't find a job to her liking. As an only child she was securing a loan from her parents to start up this café in the college town. She mentioned that since considering this business, she had difficulty sleeping and eating because of her overwhelming fear. I recommended that we discuss this further with her parents. A series of questions at this meeting revealed that while she had some academic business skills, she had no culinary background and no hands-on experience in a related food business. My recommendations were that Barbara get a temporary job in a similar café, learn the essential business and management skills, save 15% of her salary to plug into the business and return in a year to talk further. Barbara gave a sigh of relief and agreed on this proposal. She secured a job, began working on her BAP and in one year she was back, eager to start the College Coffee Café. It had been a great day when she came into my office to inquire about the price of a scone and a cup of coffee.

After settling on the nature you wish your inventory to be you must find your suppliers. The most frequently asked questions by women before they start their business are, "Where do I find my particular suppliers?" Finding the appropriate supplier is not easy because you have to explore numerous resources such as the Yellow Pages, trade magazines, and perhaps, the library. You could go to a store that sells similar products and find the suppliers listed right on the product itself or on the warranty sheet.

It's vital that you learn the order-filling priorities of each of your suppliers. Some suppliers fill orders on a first in first out basis, others give first attention to the larger orders, while customers with smaller orders wait. Consequently, you should specify a cancellation date on your orders. You have the right to return goods shipped after this date to the supplier. By including such a cut-off date, you increase the probability that your orders will receive prompt attention and goods will arrive on time for your selling season.

You must also give special attention to the arriving shipments, checking to be certain that the correct amount of merchandise is delivered and that the quality of the goods matches the samples previously shown to you. Suppliers, like you, are in business to make money. If you argue with them over every bill, if you ask them to cut their prices on everything they sell you, or you fail to promptly pay them, then don't be surprised if they leave you hanging.

Before you purchase your inventory, you may want to verify the reputation of the supplier by asking other small businesses for their opinion on that particular supplier. Your competitors may refuse to respond, but others may give their opinion. Don't expect a competitor to share their supplier list, because they will not! You could try asking a similar business in another city or state and perhaps, that business would share with you because you are not competition.

One important concern of your suppliers is whether or not they will allow you to charge and pay them within thirty to sixty days. Usually, when you first open, suppliers will want to get paid cash on delivery until you build up your credibility and a sound reputation for paying your bills. This is one factor that you should address when calculating your initial start-up costs because you will probably have to pay for your entire initial inventory up front.

Loseras seldom shop around for their suppliers because they are usually too disorganized. Victorias always do because the results are good supplies at a fair price that are delivered in a timely fashion. In addition, Victorias shop around for new prices when they reorder their inventory items to ensure that they are getting the best for their dollars.

One area that you will need to check out is whether or not the suppliers charge shipping and handling. If they do, then you must add this charge to the costs. Also, inquire about what happens with damaged goods, who pays to ship them back and how long the wait is for the new replacement inventory. Many Victorias change suppliers when they are kept waiting for inventory that is quickly needed for special occasions such as Mother's Day, Valentine's Day and the holiday season.

When selecting your suppliers, consider the following:

• *How long does it take to get my supplies?*
You must have your inventory for your Grand Opening and then promptly when the need for more arises. You may need some inventory quicker than others, like the holiday seasons. You also don't want to wait around for undeliverable orders.

• *Are supplies delivered C.O.D. or can I have 30 days to pay?*

This is important because of restricted cash flow when you first start your business. Usually, most suppliers will send the initial inventory C.O.D. so you need ready cash.

• *What is the interest rate?*
Here is another item that you will have to add when you start costing out your products.

• *Do I get a discount if I buy in quantities?*
This may be an important factor if you anticipate selling a lot of one unit.

• *What are the freight costs? Who pays them?*

• *What is the supplier's policy on shipping small orders? Time frame?*
You want to know right up front if a supplier refuses to ship small orders because this may impact your ability to supply your customer who wants one item that is out of stock at your store.

• *Who pays for the shipping and handling? What is the rate?*
Shipping costs can become very costly and it is best to know this charge up front and include it in your overall customer cost.

• *What happens if goods are damaged on route? How long before a replacement?*
Many suppliers will replace damaged goods immediately at no cost. This is the firm that you are seeking.

You need to visualize your purchases on the following grid:

NAME OF SUPPLIER	ADDRESS	ITEM	DISCOUNT	FREIGHT	COST

You will need to compare your inventory and your prices with those of your competitors. Obviously your prices must compare favorably with those of your competitors, unless the quality of your goods are of decidedly superior quality in which case your prices can be higher than your competitors'. You may wish to undercut the prices of your competitors, but only if you can do so without threatening your profit margin. More customers buying your goods at lower prices may counterbalance the profit margin from individual sales. You must know who your competition will be if you are to be competitive. Then you must proceed to identify your competitors' strengths and weaknesses through intensive research.

In securing your inventory and choosing the prices you wish to charge for it, you may wish to take into consideration the international market.

Often in my career I encounter women who want to enter the international business market with their products and come to seek my advice. The main personal and business purposes for entering international business must be identified, along with specific goals that will be steps toward accomplishing overall objectives. The international activities must be compatible with the overall business goals, objectives and tasks. The goals you want to attain should include researching the growth of sales volume, profits before taxes, compensation for your work and the time that you are willing to commit.

In selecting products from your present line for distribution internationally, you should consider products that have been successfully distributed and sold here in the domestic market. In addition, the product must fill a proven need for the purchaser in the targeted foreign market in regards to function and price. Your product must be unique and something that the foreign buyers can't live without.

There are two basic methods of exporting, direct and indirect. With the direct method, you would establish within your current U.S. business complete responsibility for the international trade. This would include market research, establishing distribution networks, performing exporting functions and directly servicing the market that you have established. You should establish within your business the person responsible for the exporting activities. She needs to identify the market and develop the exporting promotional materials either in house or by using an export management consulting company that has the expertise to identify your markets and develop your specific exporting promotional strategies.

You will need international consultants and advisors including an accountant, attorney, banker who have international expertise and an international freight forwarder, an export consultant and other key international advisors. Once you have customers identified in a chosen market, then you must determine the method of distribution of your product. Perhaps, you can find out how other U.S. firms sell in the markets that you have chosen.

The other method of breaking into the international market is through the indirect method. You will seek and secure an export management company to represent you overseas. Usually, this commitment is for a minimum of one or two years. The export management company agrees to do all export promotions and you agree to provide the product at a cost equal to or below the domestic wholesale cost, deducting such items as domestic advertisement and general administrative costs.

You may also consider selling to large U.S. firms for export through their own overseas distribution networks at a cost similar to that of the export management company.

Unless you go through the indirect method, you will have to determine anticipated international overhead expenses such as legal fees, accounting fees, promotional materials, travel, freight costs, communications, advertising, promotional expenses and additional management expenses that will arise. The question that arises is whether you have the experience and expertise to use the direct method for your international business operation.

One of my previous Victorias wanted to sell her unique lamps overseas and came in to find out where to begin. She had a successful business here, selling unique lamps, one-of-a-kind figurines and some antiques. She wanted to sell her lamps in Italy. My first question was, "Are you making money here on your lamps?" She quickly replied that there was a seventy per cent markup and her profit margin consistently remained above her projections. Another question was, "What made you select Italy as an international market?" She said that her family came from Italy twenty years ago, visited family there each year and still spoke the language. She researched the indirect method and selected a large U.S. firm for exporting her lamps through their overseas distribution networks. She was happy for the first year but then decided it was too much hassle to continue because the profit margin just didn't justify all the work.

Point 8 of the BAP: Locating, Enticing and Pleasing Your Customers
After securing the proper inventory and determining the prices for your goods, you will need to turn to that point in your business where the rubber meets the road. After all, everything mentioned heretofore is in preparation for selling your goods and services to your customer. Our final point of the BAP is number 8: locate, entice and please your customers. To lure your customers into the store you will need to work on both the general area of marketing and the specific area of advertising. You will discover that marketing is a more general subject than advertising. Advertising is part of your marketing strategy. My definition of marketing is to formulate the image of your business, to define your customer base, and to locate these customers. You must have complete knowledge about your marketing plan at all times. True, you could enlist a marketing firm, but you still must have control over the ongoing progress because nobody knows more about your product or service than you do. I recommend that you research and read everything that you can about marketing. The Internet is a great way to find these resources.

Even if you hire a marketing firm, I strongly recommend that you stay in control when developing the Marketing Plan. It should cover the following:

1. Who are my customers?
2. What kind of people are they?
3. Where do they live?
4. Are we offering a product or service that they want?
5. Are prices consistent with what buyers view as product value?
6. How does your business compare with competitors?

I recommend that you use my twelve-question Marketing Check List:

1. Do I have an Annual Marketing Plan now?
2. Should I spend funds on a brochure or catalog?
3. Have I considered television?
4. Should I have a presence on the Internet?
5. Am I fully aware of your distinct image?
6. Did I query current and potential customers?
7. Do I know my customer wants and needs?
8. Am I aware of changes in the marketplace that impact business?
9. Do I have a time frame for my Marketing Plan?
10. Am I working with marketing professionals at this time?
11. Am I considering one new approach to marketing?
12. Is my marketing plan unique and exciting?

Many entrepreneurs skip over the general subject of marketing to go on to their advertisement activities, thinking that they are both the same. A good example is an entrepreneur who only advertised her handmade draperies in the local Pennysaver where the average annual income of the reader is less than $22,000. She said that she selected this paper because of its low cost advertisement. The question to ask here is, could they afford her goods and the response is probably no. Hence, her advertisement dollars were wasted.

You must be aware of what your specific customers read and what they watch on television. You must also find other ways to get their attention so that they will buy your goods. Advertisement is your way of reaching the customers that you now have identified and whose location you have discovered.

I feel that the entrepreneur who saves money by not advertising is like a person who stops a clock to save money. You must be aware that in this fast-paced business world of today, you must use a variety of advertising methods in order to make potential customers aware of your products or services. Even the most successful franchise companies never stop advertising. They continuously spend millions of dollars to support the recognition of their products or services.

You should also research the question of how much advertisement dollars are enough. Many entrepreneurs use one of the following four common methods:
1. Set aside 2% to 4% of projected sales for advertising.
2. Some start-ups guess at a figure and hope that they are on target.
3. Many count on an outside marketing firm to decide this figure.
4. Successful Victorias spend more initially on advertisement to get the name of the company out there, then slack off a bit.

I find that most Victorias give their advertisement a valid test that determines its impact on sales and on the bottom line profits. Victorias start with a specific budget that will allow them to get their message across to a target group at least a dozen times. Victorias feel that it helps to get their potential customers' attention by repeating the ad, because only then will the message sink in. It is thought that the first time an ad runs, it's usually forgotten, the second time it is given some recognition and by the forth or fifth time, the reader thinks perhaps, your ad may have some validity.

Victorias appear to understand that it takes repeated exposure for customers to notice a product and ultimately, buy their products or services. At first Victorias may be disappointed in the results, but they don't quit and most of them commit to spending even more on advertising! If the advertising fails to produce customers, then Victorias go back to the drawing board and develop a new strategy for reaching customers.

Many entrepreneurs ask me what are the most effective ways to advertise? There are numerous strategies to advertise including billboards, print media, flyers, television, trade magazines, radio, the Yellow Pages, brochures, direct mailings and signs on your vehicles. I recommend the use of a variety of advertisement strategies. Once a winning advertisement campaign has been discovered, I urge you to stick to it and have a "don't fix it if it isn't broken" attitude.

"We tried it and it didn't work" is a common statement by Loseras when asked if they advertised their products or services. In most cases, a single failed advertising attempt makes the Loseras believe this form of building their business is not for them.

Let's research a failing Losera scenario at advertising. Usually, a new business owner gets excited over advertising for the very first time. She comes up with a modest amount of money for one ad (the Loseras never set aside enough) and then sit there waiting for customers to come pounding on their door. When the first attempt falls short, Loseras curse and vow never to advertise again because it just does not work!

Disappointed by their first failure, Loseras don't realize that not enough advertisement was done even to warrant a valid test of its potential impact on their business sales. Placing one ad in one newspaper and then saying it doesn't work is like opening your store and closing it because the first day's sales didn't meet your expectations.

When it comes to advertising, Loseras don't realize what they want, where to go and what to do after they have advertised. Victorias take advertising very seriously and set aside ample funds to kick off and maintain their advertisement strategies. Victorias know that effective advertisement takes time, creativity, adequate investments, testing and retesting and evaluating.

To Victorias, advertisement initiatives are like an investment in their future and like any investment, they find out all that they can about it before they decide to invest. Victorias see the value in the long-term investment in advertising, where Loseras seldom find the time or money to ever effectively advertise.

Effective advertisement includes who you are, what your products or services are, where you make your products or services and why they should buy from you. Victorias evaluate the cost of advertising, the frequency in which it should occur, what the ad will convey and how to measure the impact.

Advertisement agencies can help you plan your advertisement efforts, but you will pay. Ad agencies earn a large amount of their profits in commissions from advertisement placed on behalf of their clients. The ad costs are the same whether you or an ad agency places the ads.

Television can work for some companies. There are six elements that can work for you in a TV commercial.
   1. Store identification by keeping your logo up as much as possible.
   2. Have as much variety of merchandise as possible.
   3. Whenever possible identify brand name merchandise.
   4. Give customers a reason to act now.
   5. Make the commercial message such that the listener will get the other five elements even if the volume is turned off.
Research shows that it takes three impressions to move someone to act, that it's better to run several spots during the same part of the day than it is to run several

spots spread throughout all different parts of the day. Many Victorias tend to run two spots in the same show to increase the frequency and move the viewer to action.

One of the fallacies that Loseras cling to that I frequently hear is that they must open their business in a low key manner without much advertisement because of the fear that they will get too many customers. It is almost impossible to get Loseras to realize that they will not be overwhelmed with customers when first opening their business.

Victorias know that the Grand Opening should and must be spectacular. They write up news releases and get the local newspapers to print them free. They get the local Entrepreneur Center involved and the Center, in turn, helps to plan the entire event. The Entrepreneur Center contacts the local legislators, the Mayor and the County Executive to be at the Grand Opening. They will also invite the press for the ribbon cutting ceremony. Many times the opening is shown by the local TV station and viewed by hundreds of potential customers. All of this is free advertisement and the business is launched!

In order to measure the effectiveness of a particular advertisement strategy, Victorias continually ask their customers how and where they heard about their products or services. Never miss the opportunity to reveal how effective or ineffective the advertisement dollars are that you are spending out of your profits.

Many Victorias create an image such as the one by the Victoria Gift & Antique Shop: "Quality, Prompt Service and the Customers Come First." This is a catchy tag line that they use on their business cards and sometimes on their letterhead paper.

I recommend these eight indicators for your advertisement success:
1. Reach as many potential customers as possible.
2. Get the most people to buy.
3. Convince customers that they can't live without your product or service.
4. Get your name out there through advertising to enhance your image.
5. Convince customers that your product or service is simply the best.
6. Announce a new product or service in a big way.
7. Reinforce your continuing message.
8. Convince customers to come your way.

Everyone says that you can set up a business and sell on the Internet or on eBay, but how? Where do you begin? Being at home with a fractured ankle was the ideal time to read, explore and learn more about selling on the Web. Up-front, I will tell you that as of 2002, I had no real working knowledge about the Internet monster looming out there in the world. Thus I began my journey on learning about the Internet. Here are the results of searching for books, reading them and generating these findings.

The number one book that I would recommend to read first is *Webonomics* by Swartz, published in 1998. This is the ideal book to give you a start in learning all about the basics of the Internet.

Next you should follow up with the how to book called *Selling Online for Dummies* by Leslie Heeter Lundquist, who has worked for IBM, Apple and Xerox. This book gives you the essential information for setting up a storefront. The author covers the 10 Commandments of selling on line, 10 ways to get traffic and 10 mistakes to avoid.

Once you read the first two books and have some Internet know how, the next text is *Creating Stores on the Web* by Joe Cataudella et al, published in 1998. Joe set up and operates a very successful online video store called *Tronix*. He covers all of the steps: building online, promoting it, selling and shipping, growing your business and more. He also gives you a great list of resources.

The final book I would recommend is *Advertising on the Web* by Jim Sterne. He has authored three books about the World Wide Web and has over sixteen years experience as a Web consultant. Jim expands and covers more than the earlier texts such as; Internet laws, who's advertising and how they are advertising, what makes people click and what makes people buy. He details real stores, both the good and the bad.

Should a small business get on the Web? It is a question often asked by entrepreneurs. The Internet, particularly in its graphic interface known as the World Wide Web, is probably the most important communication vehicle developed since the telephone. The Web levels the playing field between small and big businesses.

The Web is one of the newest mediums for advertising and has an advantage over traditional advertisement techniques. The Internet makes it possible for small to medium-size businesses to compete with major ones. Of course as the Web matures, the advertisement rates will grow. Search engines are an additional method and a low cost strategy to increase awareness of your products and services. The Web allows you to communicate with your customers at their convenience. The Internet is simply a global network of computers that are connected so that people can send and receive information. You have to be connected to the global network though a server computer called Internet Service Providers, who offer connections to their servers. True, the WWW is not a panacea to small business, but it is something about which you should research and about which you should develop a written plan of action before jumping in.

There are many types of services available on the Internet such as E-mail, News and Chat groups, access to the World Wide Web, file transfer and Web site. E-mail is the most popular feature on the Internet through which you can receive, read and reply to messages. This is an electronic mail system that allows you to receive messages from an Internet mailbox address much faster than through the Post Office. You should explore whether or not this would be another way to reach your customers.

A Web site for your company could be designed to provide customers or potential customers with information about your products or services. The data is organized into what they call Web Pages, which comprise your Web site. The first page that a customer views is called your Home Page.

File Transfer makes it possible to transfer product catalogs, reports, articles, customer statistics and more to your printer, diskette or computer. Some files may be too big to transfer, so you may need a good zipping software application that will help to compress and save files while you are on the Internet. Later on you can decompress the file so that it's readable.

News & Chat Rooms are discussion groups that you can join to share information and to meet people with similar interests. Many times there is a theme such as sports, computers, business or more. This could become another way of talking about your product or service.

Utilizing the World Wide Web gives you access to a large collection of organized groups of multimedia documents and images stored on computers through various networks within the Internet. Each grouping of documents or images is referred to as a Web site.

After intensive research, you may decide that Internet marketing is for you. To establish a website, the following steps are necessary:
- Select a Web server to host your web site.
- Learn about the pricing schedule, both for start up and ongoing monthly fee.
- Initially, you may want to have your homepage built by an expert.
- Determine the amount and type of information about your product or

service you want to provide to your potential customers.
- Have your well-designed homepage posted on the Web and then wait for hits.

You get up by an advertised alarm clock, use name brand toothpaste, ride in a car you bought after seeing it on television, and eat at the Golden Arches. I feel that no matter what your product or service is, you have to get your message out to potential customers about what you are all about, how great you are and how they can buy from you. This appears to be an easy task, but many entrepreneurs like Losera bury their product or service under a basket, hoping that someone will pick it up and purchase their goods.

Example of Point Eight: Marketing & Advertisement. "Quality, cleanliness and customers come first" is the motto of Victoria's Gift & Antique Shop. The image of Victoria's Gift & Antique Shop is that of unique products, fair prices, friendly service and quality merchandise.

The market area includes people living within a thirty-mile radius and others visiting the mall. There will be some travelers outside the thirty-mile radius who come looking for unique gifts and rare antiques.

Extensive advertisement through the use of several marketing medias will be used immediately before the shop is opened. Initially, you should use newspapers and radio. Once the shop is opened you should prepare a TV commercial by the fifth month of operations.

At the same time, you should develop an Internet site so that you can sell gifts and antiques worldwide. You should research the use of billboards as an effective method of long lasting advertisement strategy. You will probably be approached by the mall and asked to join in their cooperative advertisement efforts and you should decide whether to respond to the overtures of the shopping mall.

Since word of mouth is a powerful advertisement tool you should continue to use this mode of advertisement from day one. If one customer recommends the shop to another person it would be a good idea to offer a reward to the customer who put in a good word for the shop. You should join the Chamber of Commerce, attending all of their after-hour events. At these events you have an excellent opportunity to distribute your own business cards. Even though some Grand Opening advertisement will be free, you should use frequent and multiple advertisement strategies just to reinforce the freebies. At the Grand Opening you might well wish to offer special drawings for gifts and a 20% discount throughout the shop during the first week.

During the first three months, you will want to allocate $3,000 to be spent on your initial advertisement. It is a good idea to ask customers where they heard about the shop and record what advertisement techniques were the most effective.

Even though Victoria may stock her store with excellent merchandise, and even though she may advertise the store effectively, the business will fail if the service the customers receive once they get to the store falls short of pleasing customers.

A business should focus on the long-term relationship with the customer. While an individual sale is important it is even more important to please the buyer so that he will become a long-term customer. Once the Victorias have customers, they then implement certain strategies to keep them. The Victorias customerize their business operation by maintaining the ability to react positively to a series of eight assumptions about their customers and everything that impacts their satisfaction.

8 Rules for Customer Awareness:
1. Do I really know what my customers want now and in the future? I must be fully aware of the specific market niche that I'm going after.
2. Does every person in my company know what our customers want? Knowing what your customer wants must be embedded into every fiber of your company.
3. Do we have many customers as we want? In order to be a growth-oriented company, we must keep the customer base healthy and growing. Everyone in Victoria companies from the bottom up must know customers are made of gold and if we have them we have a gold mine. The engine that generates the profits is the customer.
4. A critical element of your company's growth is increased sales. Each business opportunity needs to be maximized by leveraging the entire staff to bring it totally accountable at the point of each and every customer contact.
5. If you can't read customers' minds, then listen to what they are saying. Unless you are constantly tuned into your customers' signals, you may be missing out on messages that could bring you growth.
6. Getting the message of what your customers want is not enough. You have to be able to react rapidly to new market cues with new products or services or profits will be lost.
7. Never underestimate the information that you get from your customers. Imagine the advantage of transforming information into customer-generating profits. Although Victorias keep an eye on profits, this is often

secondary to their goal of satisfying their customers.

8. According to Victorias, businesses are built on customers and without them there will be no profit. It's as simple as that to Victorias and it is the rule by which they live and thrive. Victorias tend to have a compulsive desire to succeed.

Many women entrepreneurs forget that their customers' needs are why they are in business. Customers are the ones who generate profits. First and foremost is to find a need and satisfy it. Then Victoria should constantly ask her customers, "How am I doing?" In addition, Victoria asks what the customer's needs are and how she can meet them now or in the future. A poll on customer satisfaction would be useful.

From the moment the customer approaches your business establishment until she departs, her experience should be a pleasant one. The front window display needs to be eye-catching and tasteful. When the customer enters the store, she should receive a pleasant sensation. Some Victorias provide a subdued scent while most Victorias present subdued music that compliments the taste of her customers. Of course, the arrangement inside the store should also be eye-catching and attractive. Victorias realize that the placement of goods can be strategic. Perhaps she would want to put the more quality and expensive goods at eye level.

If the customer wishes to economize, then she will have to make that deliberate choice. Of course, the salespeople will be gracious both in dress and demeanor. It helps to greet the customer as she enters the store; it helps even more if the salesperson can call the customer by his or her name. It may be helpful if the salesperson can inform the customer that she can assist her in finding what she needs. Of course, the salesperson will have all the knowledge of the merchandise at her fingertips in case the customer needs such assistance. Without hovering or pressuring the customer, the salesperson can suggest an alternative if the customer does not find exactly what she is looking for. Often a customer may feel a bit guilty about the purchase of an item. The salesperson can then encourage the customer that she has made a wise decision in purchasing the item at hand. When the customer is ready to pay for her purchase, the company policy for payment should be in place. Victoria needs to decide whether she will accept credit cards, checks, or cash only. Victoria will probably not want to get into business of letting the customer buy on credit. Often stores have layaway policies if the customer does not have the cash at hand. As pleasant and helpful as the store can be in meeting the customer's needs, complaints and disappointments will likely occur. When you first start your business operation, I recommend that you document all customer dissatisfaction and discuss this at length because it is five times harder to replace a customer than to keep the existing ones happy. Proceed with changing dissatisfied customers into extremely satisfied customers because one irate customer tells at least ten of her friends and these ten tell another ten people. All clerks should be advised of company policy for handling such matters as returns or circumstances such as the customers accidentally damaging merchandise.

I suggest that you develop a manual on how to handle an irate customer. Then you can train yourself and your employees on how to use these techniques. Here are six basic rules to build your customer manual on that work:
- Talk to the customer immediately about their complaint.
- Listen to the customer and don't interrupt.
- Ask the customer what should be done about this.
- Again, listen carefully.
- Do something immediately to satisfy this customer.
- "Thank you" is what you want to hear and the result is a happy customer.

Now many times, customers will want nothing more than for you to listen because they are venting their anger. I personally would do something nice or give them something in appreciation for their loyalty to stay with you.

Recently, I had the experience of buying a new camera from a local appliance store. After using it twice, it was quite clear that the camera was defective and so I returned it. When I went to leave it with an employee, she took the camera and threw it on a shelf. I remarked that this was no way to handle such a piece of equipment, but she just grunted and walked away. At this time, no one in charge was available in the store, so I left. The following day, I received a call from the employee stating that the lens was defective and would be replaced at a cost. In addition, she said that there was damage to the outside of the camera that would require new parts that I would have to pay for. Immediately, I knew that the outside damage was not my fault and I asked that the owner call me. I prepared to fight the battle of getting my camera fixed at no cost. The call came immediately, and the first question that the owner asked was; what would I like her to do to fix my problem. This caught me off guard, so I said that I wanted a new camera. She immediately, said fine. I could come in and pick it up any time and there would also be an upgrade for my inconvenience. Amazed, I asked why she would go to such lengths to keep me happy. She laughed and replied that I had purchased a refrigerator, stove and microwave at her store in the last three months and she wanted to keep me coming back. Now I know why this store is so successful and it would be smart for other owners to follow her example.

CHAPTER FIVE
Composing the BAP Document

Throughout the preceding chapters the points of the BAP have been presented and each has been elaborated on at length. The ball is now in your court. It is time for your response to the points of the BAP. These responses need to be a formal, written evaluation of how you intend to personalize the general principles of the BAP for your own venture. Until you do so, the BAP will simply be idle theory. Writing your response in articulate sentences has two purposes. First, it will force you to think through and put into language your response. The second purpose is that your written response will be the document that you can present to all those whose help you will need in creating the business. It is important that you create a formal and neat document for the presentation of your business that you intend to have. You will need to purchase a notebook cover that is attractive and serviceable. The first page should be considered more or less as a title page. It will say something like, *"The Business Action Plan for Company X"*. Also on this title page as author of this proposal you will place the business address, your own phone number, fax number and email address. The date of the completion of the document should be placed on the first page. All of the 8 Points on your BAP should be in bold type. Under the main headings there will appear several subheadings. To each of these you should respond with at least one complete sentence and up to ten sentences. Of course, these responses should be typed and proof-read. Your use of the English language will say a great deal about you and your proposed company.

Loseras mistakenly believe that the BAP can be stored in her head and delivered extemporaneously to those she needs to assist in getting her company started. Victorias can speak extemporaneously of course, but they will also have the written formulation of their thoughts. In fact, having written this response to the BAP, their extemporaneous speech will be all the better.

BAP Point 1:
The nature, purpose and location of the new business venture.
- A description of the exact nature of the business
- The image that will reflect the nature and uniqueness of this venture
- The legal requirements for the establishment of this venture
- Reasons for selecting this location

BAP Point 2:
Prospective customers to be serviced:
- Age, cultural background, financial status and educational background of the customer base
- The area that the business will serve
- The unique (services and products) advantage the business will offer its customers

BAP Point 3:
The financial arrangements for starting up the business:
- List projected costs for initiating the business
- Provision for ongoing regular business expenses
- Total calculation of needed costs for starting the business
- Projected sources of securing these finances
- Proposed method of reimbursing money borrowed

BAP Point 4:
Owner Profile:
- Formal education and/or previous business experience
- Characteristics of successful businesswomen that you possess
- Characteristics of unsuccessful businesswomen that you do not possess or are working to correct
- An evaluation of your personality traits that are strengths for managing a business
- Areas of weakness that you will compensate for by securing assistance

BAP Point 5:
An assessment of competition for this business venture:
- Names of competitors and the location of their businesses
- Strengths of these competitors
- Weaknesses of these competitors
- Rational for starting up a new business in light of the competition
- Reasons for the failure of those businesses that no longer exist

The BAP is your communication tool when you need to orient employees, sales personnel, suppliers and others about your operations. This plan develops you as a strong and focused business leader and manager. It can give you practice in thinking about competitive conditions, opportunities, threats, your ongoing cash flow status and situations that can make you a "Giant" in the business world of tomorrow.

The entire process and your Business Action Plan are aimed at making profits. I sense that successful women feel responsible for their own money, depend on no one else to pay their bills and believe that money buys power in the business arena.

BAP Point 6:
Deciding on management procedures for running the business:
- Time management
- Organizing the office
- Maintaining financial records so that you have adequate cash flow
- Developing an annual strategic plan
- Delegating responsibility
- Organizing meetings
- Handling stress
- Balancing domestic duties and work
- Networking
- Hiring

BAP Point 7:
The selection and handling of inventory:
- Choosing inventory
- Pricing the inventory
- Deciding on whether to venture into international business

BAP Point 8:
Locate, entice, and please your customers:
- Creating a marketing plan
- Developing an advertising program
- Develop strategies to please your customers

If you have spent years thinking that your life isn't good enough and no one appreciates all of your hard work, then perhaps, starting your own business and becoming your own boss is truly a mission you should undertake. Do yourself a favor, read this book and use the helpful hints to start planning your own business and becoming a Victoria.

I predict that your new entrepreneurial world will bring you to the highest point of happiness, satisfaction, inspiration, creativity and a love for life that you have never known before. You will never think of being employed by someone else because work will become play and everyday you will be eagerly anticipating the next exciting challenge.

Remember that there are women who make things happen, watch things happen and wonder what the heck happened…*which one are you?*

Glossary

Accounts Payable: A list of current debts or liabilities of a company.

Accounts Receivable: A list of the amounts a firm is owed by others for merchandise or services, representing current assets.

Advertisement: Strategies for reaching your customers.

Angel Investor: Individuals who invest in a company in the hopes of making a profit.

Assets: Cash or other items that will normally turn into cash

Balance Sheet: A detailed listing of assets, liabilities and owner equity accounts showing the financial position of a company.

Break-Even Analysis: The level of sales at which your total sales covers your total costs and operating expenses.

Burnout: Long term stress that if left unresolved will result in burnout.

Capital: Those funds that are needed for the base of the business.

Cash Flow: The actual movement of cash within a business.

Collateral: Property or other assets pledged by a borrower to secure a loan.

Copyright: Protection for an original work of authorship.

Current Liabilities: Amounts owed that will normally be paid off within a year.

Current Ratio: A ratio of the company's current assets to current liabilities.

Customerization: An awareness and action plan to effectively satisfy your customers' needs and desires.

Equity: The owner's investment in the company.

Equity Funds: You sell an interest in your business and this type of money is usually not repaid.

Financial Statements: see *Income Statement*.

Fixed Assets: Those items of a permanent nature required for the normal conduct of business.

Fixed Monthly Expenses: Expenditures that occur regularly every month.

Forecast: A management tool and a plan, with strategies for achieving results in your business.

Goal: A wish put to writing and usually not measurable.

Gross Profits: Net sales minus the costs of goods or services sold.

Income Statement: Scorecards that show the financial condition of your business. The income statement is also called a profit and loss statement.

Long Term Credit: Usually a loan of more than a year that is needed for expansion. This is similar to a mortgage or a promissory note with terms.

Marketing: Research strategies used in identifying your customers.

Mentor: Someone you can turn to for advice.

Motivation: An action process that encompasses the person as a whole aimed at creating positive change in the person.

Net Worth: The owner's equity in a given business represented by the excess of total assets over the total amount owed to outside creditors at a given moment in time. The net worth of an individual is determined by deducting the amount of all personal liabilities for the total value of personal assets.

Objective: Something that you want to achieve and is measurable.

Profit: The excess of the selling price over all costs and expenses.

Secured Loan: A loan for which the lender's interest is protected by collateral.

Short-Term Credit: Lenders provide a type of money for a special reason such as the purchase of inventory for next season and it's usually repaid in less than a year.

Stress: Pressures on the outside causing you problems on the inside.

Term Loan: Either secured or unsecured, usually for periods of more than one year to as many as twenty. Term loans are paid off like a mortgage.

Three Year Cash Flow Projection: A "guesstimate" of your business operation over a period of three years.

Trade Money: Money that you owe your suppliers.

Venture Capitalist: This differs from a bank. A firm that buys into your company and owns a piece of your business, with the hopes of making money.

Working Capital: The difference between current assets and current liabilities. Working capital cycles through your business in a variety of forms such as inventory, accounts and notes receivable, cash and securities.

Notes by the Reader

Notes by the Reader